This Man's
Wee Boy

This Man's Wee Boy

A Childhood Memoir of Peace and Trouble in Derry

TONY DOHERTY

MERCIER PRESS

IRISH PUBLISHER – IRISH STORY

To the memory of young Damien Harkin

MERCIER PRESS
Cork
www.mercierpress.ie

© Tony Doherty, 2016

ISBN: 978 1 78117 458 6

10 9 8 7 6 5 4 3 2 1

A CIP record for this title is available from the British Library

Printed and bound in the EU.

CONTENTS

A map of Tony's home area in 1961.
Courtesy of Ordnance Survey Ireland

Acknowledgements

There are a number of people who deserve thanks and credit. First, my wife Stephanie, for her support and patience, but especially for her belief in what I had set out to do; my mother Eileen, who, in the months before she died in August 2014, largely unknown to her, provided me with the rich pickings of our family history from her own memory bank; my big sister Karen, my wee brother Paul and my Uncle Eugene, who helped me bring our households in Moore Street and Hamilton Street back to life; my Aunt Maureen, for helping me out with the McFredericks; Dave Duggan, for telling me what to write about and how to do it; Lily (née Lily White) and Eddie Harkin, for allowing me to write about their son, Damien; Seán McLaughlin of the *Derry Journal*, for publishing 'The Folded Newspaper'; Rónán McConnell of Derry City and Strabane District Council, for sourcing the Ordnance Survey map; Mickey Dobbins, Amanda Doherty and Julieann Campbell, for their prompt and honest feedback and encouragement; Minty Thompson, the oracle of every seed, breed and generation in the Brandywell; both Conal McFeely of Creggan Enterprises and the Trustees of the Bloody Sunday Trust, for helping me; Felicity McCaul, the godmother of The Literary Ladies, including Freya and Lynne; and Averill Buchanan for her skilful editing and her insightful feedback and guidance. Finally, thanks to my kitchen table and the two red robins, Maureen and Patrick, who came to my doorstep in the early spring and summer mornings. Maureen was there for a nosey and Patrick to practise his cursing.

Tony Doherty

1

MOORE STREET, 1967–68

My father ('me da') was at the open front door, standing between me and the sunny street. He was smoking and he looked up and down the street while I stood behind him in the darkened hall with my homemade drum hanging from a cord around my neck. Earlier he had made holes in the sides of a square biscuit tin with a screwdriver to knot the cord through. I had a wooden stick in each hand.

The marching band was forming under the sun in the middle of the street, halfway between our house and McKinneys' across from us, mostly boys with one girl. Our instruments were sweet tins and biscuit tins; one had a family-size Heinz Beans tin. Some, like me, had their drums hanging around their necks; others just carried the tins in their hands. Our drumsticks were the kindling sticks used for lighting the fire in the house. The band gathered in the street, banging, clanging, clunking, raring to go.

As me da stood in the doorway the sound of a car could be heard coming to a quick stop at the bottom of the street.

'What are these cowboys at now?' said me da out loud

to no one in particular. He stood down from the front step onto the street and I squeezed past him to join the band. At the bottom of the street two policemen got out of their car and one took a football from three older boys who had been playing there.

'Hi!' called me da, slowly making his way towards them. He had his beige shirtsleeves turned up as usual. 'Hi! What the hell are yous boys at there wi' them fellas?' He stopped about twenty yards away from them and then began walking towards them again more slowly.

The dark-uniformed policemen looked unsure of themselves as he approached. The marching band stopped drumming. There was complete silence in the terraced street.

'The days of yous boys messing wains about are over. Give them back their ball and get the fuck from this street!' Me da was desperate with his temper when he started.

The policemen looked even more uncomfortable. The lanky one whispered something to the one with the ball in his hands, who promptly threw the ball back to the teenagers. None of them said anything.

Me da lowered his voice but you could hear him say, almost in a whisper, 'Now fuck off into your fancy car and get the fuck out and don't come back here messin' people about.' He pointed with his thumb towards the end of the road as he spoke each word.

The two policemen did exactly as they were told and drove

off up the Foyle Road in the direction of Killea. Still puffing on his Park Drive fag, me da turned around with a broad grin on his face and walked slowly back towards the house. The teenagers went back to playing football.

Off the band went in single file up Moore Street. Me, our Patrick and Paul, Ernie Thompson, Dooter and Jacqueline McKinney and their dog Dandy – Dandy McKinney, one of the family. We all wore shorts and stripy t-shirts, and our plastic sandals of blue, brown and red made a sharp split-splat sound on the hard, dusty ground as we marched. I was at the back and Dooter walked in front of me. He wore red rubber boots that were too big for him so he flip-flopped about and staggered a bit as he walked.

The short-back-and-sides heads with wing-nutted ears bobbed in and out of the line in front of me as we walked in formation, banging the drums with our wooden sticks and making a noise that bore no relationship to the tunes we thought we were playing: 'We all live in a yella submarine, a yella submarine, a yella submarine.' *Clunk, clunk, bang, bang – clunk, bang, clunk, bang.*

As it was a sunny day some of the houses had their front doors open; there were prams outside with babies in them taking in the sun and fresh air. We passed Wee Mary's house on the left near the top. Wee Mary would invite us in now and again. She lived on her own with her cats and didn't say a lot. She just pointed and gestured and said some words

11

now and again. Wee Mary Fleabag, some in the street called her.

On the other side, Barry McCool had Peggy the horse out of the stable and was brushing down her snow-white coat in the sun at the bottom of the steep bankin'. Barry smiled at us as we passed his stable. So did Peggy the horse.

At the top of Moore Street you come to waste ground. You turn right to go up the steep bankin' or left to go down to-wards Hamilton Street, where you come out between the two gable-ends. Down we went: 'Here we come, walking down the street.' *Clunk, clunk, bang, bang – clunk, bang, clunk, bang.*

As we reached Hamilton Street we swung left and walked Indian file past Chesty Crossan, who was sitting on his kitchen chair in the shade in front of his cottage in his white string vest. He smiled as we passed, battering our drums and chanting the lines from The Monkees that we knew and humming the ones we didn't.

'Hello, Chesty!' called our Paul.

'Hello, wee Doherty!' Chesty called back with a laugh.

Hamilton Street was longer than Moore Street, bending gradually almost out of sight towards Quarry Street, Lecky Road and the Bogside, which was out of bounds for us. The houses were all painted dull or pastel shades, with the odd splash of red or yellow on the windowsills to brighten them in the sunshine. The Barbours were playing tig in front of their house. As we passed, Johnny Barbour abandoned the game and took up position behind me. He had no drum, but he walked in formation with the marching band and sang what he knew.

We passed McLaughlin's shop, with its grey walls and darkened insides, and then the Silver Dog bar near the corner. On the wooden bench outside a solitary, old, flat-capped man was sitting with a glass of stout in his hand. He smiled, raised his glass and said, 'Good on yis boys', as we passed by. As we reached the end of Hamilton Street and turned left onto Foyle Road, our Patrick said, 'Get on the pad', and led us towards the footpath. Foyle Road was busier than Hamilton Street. This was the bottom of Bishop Street, where the Morrisons and Thompsons lived. They weren't part of the hated Bishie Gang because they lived at the bottom of Bishop Street, just around the corner from us. The real Bishie Gang all lived further up Bishop Street, out of view from our street. Kevin Morrison joined our band. He had no drum either but fell in behind Johnny Barbour as we made our way towards the corner of Moore Street again.

Mrs Thompson was out in her apron brushing the dirt and dust off her step. Her black hair was up in a bun on top of her head. She smiled as we passed and rested on her brush for a moment watching us make another go of 'The Yellow Submarine'. She was Ernie's ma.

The teenagers were still at the corner playing football and made way for us to get back to where we started. At that moment, a small blue van pulled into Moore Street just in front of us and stopped. The door opened and the Fishman got out. He had jet-black curly hair like me da's and wore blue overalls.

'Fresh herrin'!' he shouted. 'Fresh herrin'!'

The band stopped to watch. He opened the back doors of the van to reveal fresh fish packed in boxes. We could smell it from where we were standing. Women came out of their houses with coloured scarves on their heads. Paddy Stewart came out of ours with his flat cap on his head. The women paid their money and got their fresh herring wrapped in newspaper, chatted for a few minutes and went back indoors again. The Fishman closed the back doors, got back into the van and drove off down the lane to Hamilton Street. The band started up again and hurried down the lane after him, calling 'Fresh herrin'! Fresh herrin'!' at the tops of our voices and beating our drums ferociously. Dooter fell over in his red floppy boots and he and his drum clattered to the ground. Up he got, brushed the dust off his bare legs, and on we went. In Hamilton Street more women came out with coloured scarves on their heads, bought their fish, chatted and went back in again. The wee blue van drove off towards Anne Street below where me granny and granda Doherty lived in the prefabs.

The marching band broke up in Hamilton Street, where we joined the Barbours playing tig, running away from whoever was 'it', and declaring 'parley' by touching a lamp post with both hands so you couldn't be caught and you could get your breath back. After the tig we sat down in the sun on the kerb opposite Chesty, still sitting in his kitchen chair at his front door.

I spied a patch of dull-pink chewing gum stuck to the road and poked at it with an ice-pop stick to see if it would move. Softened by the heat, it came away easily in pinky-white strings.

'Hi, I got chewin' gum! Look!' I shouted.

'What is it?' asked Johnny Barbour.

'It's a Bubbly,' I said, rolling it in my fingers. I kissed it up to God and put it in my mouth. There was still a bit of flavour off it, as well as a few pieces of grit, which I picked out in a pincer movement with my tongue and fingers.

'Gis that ice-pop stick,' said Johnny.

I threw him the ice-pop stick and he poked at a piece of dull-white chewing gum near his feet. It came up in strings too. The sun was a blessing for chewing gum. He rolled it in his fingers, kissed it and held it up to the sky.

'I kiss this up to God,' he said and promptly stuck it in his mouth.

'What kind did you get, Johnny?' I asked.

'Beechnut,' he said with a smile, crunching on a bit of grit, as I had.

'It's okay when you kiss it up to God, isn't it?' said our Paul, sitting down beside Johnny.

15

'Aye, it is. As long as you kiss it up to God you won't get poisoned,' I said and watched our Paul poke another dull-pink Bubbly with the stick.

* * *

It was our first day at school. The classroom at Long Tower Primary School had erupted with four-year-olds crying for their mammies. Mrs Radcliffe was being stern with some of the mothers who were in the classroom. They had to leave. They were only making the children worse. Almost all of the thirty boys were crying like babies and I wondered what they were crying about. I was the only boy in the class not crying. It took a long time to get the mammies out the door. They stood outside looking in through the glass at all the wains crying. Then some of the mammies started to cry. Mrs Radcliffe went out to them, closing the door behind her. Eventually they dried their eyes and left. Mrs Radcliffe was always stern. When school finished later that day they were all back, crying again in the yard. The mammies had their boys by the hand or were hugging them.

Only a few boys cried on the second day, but one of them cacked himself in the classroom. Mrs Radcliffe was purple-faced. She took him out to the toilet. When they came back he was wearing someone else's trousers. We all got a small bottle of cold milk in the morning. Some boys didn't drink their milk but Mrs Radcliffe said you had to, to make your bones and teeth strong. They only sipped it. I drank the whole bottle as I wanted to have strong bones and teeth. I had toast wrapped in bread-paper for lunch. The two slices of cold toast were really nice because the butter had caramelised with the burnt bits. We got hot tea with sugar at lunchtime. Mrs Radcliffe poured it for us from a giant silver teapot into cups and small milk bottles.

I went home with our Patrick and Karen. Karen was a big girl in Primary Three in the Long Tower Girls' School.

On the way home one day our Patrick said to me, 'You're deef.'

I said, 'What?' and he said, 'I said, "You're deef."'

'What d'ye mean, deef?' I asked.

'Me ma said to Paddy Stewart the other day that she thought you couldn't hear right, and Paddy said that you might be a bit deef all right,' he said.

'But I'm not deef. Sure I can hear ye talkin'!' I said, feeling a bit hard done by.

'Well, that's what they said. You're deef and that's it!'

'Naw, I'm not deef! I'm not, aren't I not, Karen?' I asked, alarmed and looking for another opinion.

'Naw you're not. Patrick, stop you narking him,' she replied.

'I'm only tellin' yis what they said. It was Paddy Stewart that said you're deef,' said Patrick.

'Well, give over about it now,' said Karen and we walked home in silence.

A day or two later me ma called into the school to get me out early. She was standing in the corridor when Mrs Radcliffe said that I had to go. We walked from the Long Tower School towards Abercorn Road where Riverview House was. As we walked me ma said she had to get an hour off work in the factory to take me to get a hearing test.

'I'm not deaf, Ma, amn't I not?' I asked, looking up to her face to see her reaction.

'Och naw, son,' she said, with an anxious smile back at me. 'Everybody gits an ear test when they're young.'

'Everybody in the class?' I asked.

'Aye, you're the first. Aren't you the lucky wan?'

When we got to Riverview House we were taken by a smiling, blue-uniformed nurse into a cream-painted room with two wooden chairs and a wooden table with a wooden mallet on it and a pair of black metal earphones wired into a grey metal box on the wall above the table. The nurse explained that I was to put the earphones on my head, she would go out of the room and that I was to tap the table with the wooden mallet after I heard a beep on the earphones. Me ma sat down at the table opposite a large, square window looking into another room, behind which the nurse would sit down. I was to sit facing away from the window. The nurse placed the earphones over my head, covering both ears. I couldn't hear a thing from this point on and wondered was I supposed to be hearing beeps or was I really going deaf. I had the mallet in a death-grip, and had heard nothing yet from the earphones. I waited … and waited a few seconds more …

I heard a very faint beep. A weak one but I definitely heard it! I raised the mallet and brought it down hard on the table with all the strength of a boy worried about going deaf. Bang! Me ma, who had been looking in at the nurse and not at me, screamed 'Jesus Christ!' at the top of her voice, jumped up from her chair, her handbag fell off her knees onto the floor and all her belongings fell across the floor. Papers and lipstick everywhere. The nurse rushed in from the windowed room next door and said, 'Are you okay, Mrs Doherty?' I could only hear the talk in muffles. Me ma sat back down on her wooden chair, put her hands over her face, and her shoulders started heaving. I thought she was crying into her hands but then I heard the laughs of her and, when she took her hands away, her eyes ran black with make-up.

'Jesus, Tony Doherty!' she said, still laughing. 'You're goney bring on a heart attack!' The nurse and me ma got down on their hunkers to lift all me ma's things from the floor. Me ma then placed the handbag squarely on the table.

'I know, Tony,' the nurse said, smiling and patting my hand after she lifted the earphones from my head. 'Just hit the table a wee tap so I can see your hand moving through the window.' She placed the earphones over my ears again and returned to the other room. My knuckled grip on the mallet remained strong, despite the nurse's advice. I had the earphones on and could hear nothing. So I waited ... me ma, her still giggling and looking at me this time, put her hands up to her ears. I waited ...

I heard another very weak beep. Weaker than the first one but definitely a beep! Again, I brought the mallet down hard on the wooden table with all my strength. Bang! Me ma, who had been watching me this time, put her hands round to cover her open mouth as she looked, wide-eyed, in through the window at the nurse. The nurse came in again from the other room, gently lifted the black earphones off my head and said, 'Mrs Doherty, there's not a thing wrong with this boy's ears, but could you take him out of here before he wrecks the place!' My grip on the mallet released at the news and I put my hands down by my sides.

'Oh dear, nurse, I'm really mortified,' said me ma, who was still wiping the black make-up from her eyes with a hankie.

'That's okay, Mrs Doherty. He's a wile man, that 'un!' said the nurse, smiling back at us.

'Och, I know. He'd get ye hung!' laughed me ma as we went out through the large wooden doors.

'I'm not deaf, Ma. Aren't I not?' I asked her again as we climbed the stone steps up to Abercorn Park.

'Naw, you're not at all, son. You're just in a world of your own sometimes.'

I wondered what she meant as we passed the swings and slides towards home.

I'm not deef and that's the main thing! I thought to myself and couldn't wait to get home to tell our Patrick.

* * *

Paul started Primary One in September 1968. The four of us walked home together down Bishop Street. There were Daz washing powder promotion coupons posted in the doors the whole way down the street. We pulled them out of the flaps. They were currency in the shop. We cut in from Bishop Street, dandered around the base of the bankin' and went in through the back gate to the whitewashed yard with the toilet. It always smelled of a mixture of farts and old damp newspaper.

Paddy Stewart – Uncle Paddy – stood proudly in our kitchen as we filed in the door. 'Your dinner's ready,' he said.

The dinner was in bowls keeping warm on top of the range. There was a light skin on the beans, which made them even nicer. Beans, sausages and mashed spuds with butter. Paddy wasn't really our uncle but he came with the house. He lifted the bowls with a towel over to the drop-leaf table in the scullery and salted the food for us. We tore into it with spoons.

'Was school good the day, Paul?' he asked. Paul was his favourite, you could tell.

'We got all the Daz coupons coming down Bishop Street,' announced Paul.

'That's great son, that ye got the coupons.'

Paddy was sitting drinking a cup of tea on the chaise longue while we ate. He was a lovable man with his round belly and red nose.

'Paddy, me da said that ye played for Derry. Did ye?' I asked from the table.

'Oh aye, I did surely. Me and me brother Gerry. Played in the Brandywell, and up and down the country. That was years ago. I wouldn't be fit now to kick football, boys-a-boys,' Paddy laughed.

When we were playing out the back lane we used to pee ourselves laughing when Paddy went to the toilet in the yard. 'Wait d'ye hear the blatters of this. Paddy's in the shite house,' we'd whisper to each other. And sure enough, Paddy would oblige, as loud and proud a blatter of farts that you ever heard.

* * *

Me ma worked in a shirt factory. One morning I saw her from our doorstep getting on a bus on the Foyle Road at the bottom of Moore Street. I never knew she got a bus to work and was excited by this. I called out to her but she didn't hear me. I ran down Moore Street, waving, until I reached the bottom. All the women in the bus were laughing and waving back. I saw me ma walking up the bus and stooping down to look at the waving boy. She waved back and laughed. I didn't know why they were laughing.

Our house was really dootsy and old-fashioned. The only

new things were the black plastic settee and matching chairs in the front room. The cushions were a fiery orange. We had square-patterned oilcloth all over the downstairs floor and on the stairs themselves. It was very worn in the hall. You could see the black stuff coming through where the pattern had worn away. There were two blue-and-white dogs that sat high up on the wooden mantelpiece, one on either side of an old brown clock with a yellowed face. We were No. 6 Moore Street, the house with the dull-green door and the heavy brass knocker. Other knockers on the doors in Moore Street were shiny. Ours wasn't.

The McKinneys lived across the street. They had a van because their da, Cecil, had greyhounds. He was a doggy-man. Cecil and the McKinneys' Uncle Davy kept the dogs in sheds up the bankin' up near the College. We were allowed to walk the dogs out the Line with Terry, who was older by two or three years and knew everything. The Line was a disused railway track which ran the full length of our side of the River Foyle. Sometimes we were allowed to go to the dog races at Lifford Stadium. We'd travel in the back of the van with the dogs. We got chips and coke and learned how to gamble. You got a coloured ticket when you bet. My favourite dog was DC Wonder. DC stood for Derry City. She was a big, fawn dog. Nearly all Cecil's dogs were called something or other Wonder, such as Joan's Wonder, The Third Wonder and The Eleventh Wonder, although one was called Teresa's Pride after Dooter's wee sister and Cecil and Maisie's youngest daughter.

Dooter was called Dooter because, when he was a toddler, he couldn't say his name right. His real name was Christopher but he could only say something like Dooter and it stuck, though his ma and da still called him Christopher.

The McKinneys were the same ages as us. Our Karen was the same age as Terry McKinney; our Patrick, named after me da, was the same age as Michael McKinney; I was the same age as Jacqueline McKinney who, it was rumoured, was my girlfriend; and our Paul was the same age as Dooter. After Paul the Dohertys stopped for a while, but the McKinneys kept on coming – there were Teresa and Don. They weren't the same age as anyone so didn't really count. They had Dandy the dog, though. She did count. We had no dog. We used to sing:

> Doherty's sausages bad for your heart, the more you eat the more you fart!
>
> Doherty's sausages bad for your heart, the more you eat the more you fart!
>
> McKinney's tea, makes your granny pee!
>
> McKinney's tea, makes your granny pee!

There was no McKinney's tea. But there were Doherty's sausages.

* * *

It was my fifth birthday. My birthday was exactly a week after Christmas Day – on 1 January. (I was born just after midnight, me ma said, in the front bedroom of me granny Quigley's house in Central Drive during a terrible storm.) There was no money to do anything special for my birthday; they had spent it all at Christmas. But Karen was sent to the shop for a Swiss Roll and a bottle of Cloudy Lime. The Cloudy Lime was poured into cups and me ma stuck five candles in the Swiss Roll and lit them.

'Blow them out and make a wish,' she said as we sat around the coffee table in the front room on New Year's Day.

I did. I wished for something for my birthday.

'We'll get you something when we get paid,' said me ma, looking at me da. 'Isn't that right, Paddy?'

'It is surely, Eileen,' he said with a smile.

Me da usually got paid on a Friday. I think me ma did as well. On payday we got our own pay from me da when he got home from work. Me ma didn't pay us. We'd wait for him coming across the waste ground at the top of Moore Street and run to meet him to be lifted up and get our pay when we reached the house. Sometimes he'd be late so we just played at the corner and watched out for him. If he was late you could smell the beer off him when he lifted you. He'd rub his stubbly face roughly into our necks when he had the drink in him. Once he scratched Karen on the face, he rubbed that hard. Sometimes he'd pull bars of chocolate from his work-coat pockets as we walked back towards the house – usually Marathons and Bar Sixes. Marathons made you run faster; it said so on TV. Our pay was handed over at the table – sixpence for Karen and Patrick, and fourpence for me and Paul.

We used to go and make secrets in the bankin'. Secrets could be holy medals or coloured milk bottle tops or something cut from a magazine. It didn't matter so long as it was shiny when placed against the soil. Then it was covered over with coloured glass, usually the bottom of a green bottle. The glass changed the colour of the secret. This was the secret. We went back the next day to see if the secrets were still there. They were. They looked peaceful under the green glass. We covered them and left them there for another day. You could see other people's secrets. No one kept them secret.

I had my own secret. I saved my pay in a hole in the bankin' for a number of weeks. I didn't save for any particular reason; I just saved. I didn't tell anyone. I'd just sneak off after we got our pay at the table and go round to the base of the bankin', remove the sod and stash the four big copper pennies. I covered the dull pennies over with the bottom of a Mundies wine bottle with a hollow in it. I did it for about three weeks. I had twelve large pennies to my name, blew it all on sweets and chocolate in Melaugh's shop on Hamilton Street and bought everyone in the marching band Dainties, Bubblys and Chocolate Logs. We shared a big glass bottle of

Black Cat Cola between eight of us. Black Cat Cola had a cartoon picture of a smiling black cat on the label. Black Cat Cola was the real deal.

The paydays came and went. Each school day I'd get up to see if my birthday wish had come true. Each day as I came downstairs there'd be nothing in the hall or the scullery or front room. But I kept true to my wish. One day, as we awoke for school and came downstairs, there was a big red toy bus with yellow seats parked in the hall. I ran down the stairs in delight that at last my wish had come true.

'That's not yours, Tony,' said me da, not realising. 'It's Paul's birthday the day, so it's his.'

I was devastated. This was my first big let down with my parents.

Paul came running downstairs.

'Thanks, Mammy and Daddy. This is class, hi!' he said, as he got on the bus and pushed himself up and down the hall.

I started to cry in my arms against the wall in the scullery and me ma shouted at me to stop being so selfish. 'It's your brother's birthday, not yours.'

A few nights later the red toy bus was parked outside our house.

'Dooter, jump you on and I'll push ye,' I said and Dooter jumped on.

I pushed him around the back of Moore Street below the bankin' where we came to a stop in the muck.

'Hi, Dooter,' I said, 'I'll give you half my pay this week if you do me a favour.'

'What?'

'Lift that boulder there and hit the bus wi' it,' I said.

Without any further persuasion from me he lifted the heavy round boulder and brought it down with a crash on top of the bus. Its red roof split in two and a wee yellow seat scooted out onto the grass.

'Do it again, Dooter,' I said, and he did it again.

More yellow seats shot out of the bus. Then I lifted the boulder and smashed it down hard. The bus broke in two, with yellow and red pieces of plastic scattering on the green grass. It didn't look like a bus when we left.

Away we ran back round to our street. Me da and Paul were out at the front door.

'Did ye see our Paul's bus?' me da asked.

Paul was crying. Dooter took off in his red waterboots and ran into his house and closed the door without looking back. I was on my own.

'What's wrong wi' him?' he said.

I didn't answer.

'What are yous boys up to?'

I said nothing.

But he knew. 'Did you take his bus, boy?'

I didn't answer.

'Take me around the corner!' he demanded angrily.

I was hammered and I knew it.

When we got round the corner past Barry McCool's stables to the bankin' it was all still there. It hadn't disappeared. Paul started howling the way Dandy McKinney howls at the music from the Poke Van.

'It was Dooter, Daddy. It wasn't me. I tried to stop him but he lifted that boulder there and just smashed it,' I said.

He didn't believe me. Paul was sent howling round to the house to get a box. He was still howling when he came back with the box. The tears and snotters were blinding his eyes, which looked at me and at the scene before him in disbelief at what I'd done.

'It's all right, Paul. We'll get you another bus,' said me da to get him to stop.

It didn't work. He howled on.

'You.' Me da looked straight at me. 'Put all the pieces into the box.'

I got down on my hunkers and started collecting all the broken bits of red and yellow plastic from the mucky ground.

'Right, carry it back to the house. Now.'

As I turned with the box in my arms he gave me a right steever with his boot up the backside, shoving me on a few extra yards with the force. I started to cry. The box wasn't heavy.

'You're in bother, boy,' was all he said from behind me as we walked. I knew he meant it.

When we got back to the house I put the box down on the scullery floor and then I was sent upstairs to put on my Sunday clothes. My Sunday coat was waiting for me over the chaise longue when I came down. It was brown check with chocolate brown buttons. They looked too much like chocolate to be buttons. There was a small, dull-brown attaché case with a brown leather and metal handle sitting in the hall, exactly where the bus was parked on its first day. Everyone was gathered in the scullery – Ma, Da, Paddy Stewart, Karen, Patrick and Paul. The howling had stopped and Paul was wiping his snotters into me ma. The box of broken plastic was still on the floor where I'd left it. Everyone stood around it.

'You're coming wi' me, boy,' me da said, picking up the case as we went out the door.

We walked side by side down to the bottom of Moore Street. I looked around before turning the corner and saw that they were all standing outside the house, watching. The leaving party. Our Paul was smirking at me.

'You're goin' to Termonbacca, boy,' said me da as we walked down the street. 'That was a terrible thing you done on your brother.'

Termonbacca was where Gerry Goodman lived. Gerry Goodman was in our class in school. He had no parents so he lived in Termonbacca with the nuns. He was very happy; he smiled a lot. He always wore grey long shorts and brown boots with grey socks and a navy blue blazer. All the home boys at the Long Tower wore grey trousers that went down to the knee. Gerry Goodman was going to be my best friend. I wondered what wearing long short trousers felt like.

We turned the corner onto Foyle Road and could see the lights on the hill where Termonbacca sits. Me da walked without a word and at a fast pace, but I kept up with him. I didn't know what to say so I stayed silent. Anyway he'd made his mind up, by the looks of him. He carried the attaché case. I held his hand. It was freezing. I was feeling the cold. When we reached the corner of Lone Moor Road he stopped suddenly.

'Do you want to go and live up the Coach Road with the Home Boys, Tony?' he asked.

The Coach Road! The Coach Road was so named because the Headless Coachman rode his black, horse-driven coach up and down that road in the dead of night and kidnapped children and took them away for ever.

'No, Daddy,' I said truthfully. 'I'm really sorry,' I added; that wasn't so truthful. 'I don't want to go to up the Coach Road to the Home.' I started crying. I had visions of lying in bed in the Home hearing the Headless Coachman on the road outside cracking his whip and screaming at the kidnapped wains in the coach to be quiet.

'Sorry for what?' me da asked.

'Sorry for smashing Paul's bus,' I said, lying through tears this time. 'I'll make up for it. I'll give him my pay for four weeks.'

31

'Right, I'll give you one more chance. Another stunt like that and you're for up the Coach Road. Okay?'

'All right, Daddy. I won't do it again. I'm really sorry.'

I wasn't.

We turned around and headed back towards Moore Street. Dooter was out playing in the street and ran in again when he saw us coming round the corner. When we reached the house everyone was in the scullery around the heat from the range. I was sent to bed after saying sorry to Paul and promising to pay him four weeks in a row.

That night I pictured myself being lowered into a grave and looking up to see me ma and da crying their eyes out as they looked down at me disappearing. It'd serve them right, I thought as I drifted off to sleep on my own.

* * *

One day I followed our Patrick, and Michael and Terry McKinney, round to the quarry. The u-shaped quarry was a piece of flat land below the bankin' and was full of bits of junk and car parts, and bones of dead farm animals, mostly sheep with their horns still on. The older boys wanted rid of me and kept chasing me away. Patrick swung his boot at me but missed. I tripped and stumbled and fell on the palm of my hand. Something sliced into it and when I brought it up to my face the blood was gushing from an open wound on the fleshy part near the wrist. I needed help. I started to cry and called to the boys ahead but they told me to fuck off and go back home; then they ran away. Our Patrick was a wild curser. So was Michael McKinney.

Dripping blood over my t-shirt, shorts, bare legs and socks, I made my way back to the house emitting a series of low and medium-pitched moans. It was sore but it looked worse. The open wound scared me as I could see flesh inside. Me ma and da were in the scullery.

'Jesus, what happened you, son?' me ma said, as I moaned my way in through the door.

'The big boys were chasing me away and I fell. And our Patrick was cursing at me,' I said, holding out my bloodied hand for inspection.

Me da took me to the water tap in the yard. The water stung and me ma said, 'Go easy on him, Paddy – it looks really sore.'

My cut hand was wrapped in a cut-up pillowcase and me da took me over to Altnagelvin on the bus. We got the bus on Foyle Road to Foyle Street and then got the Altnagelvin bus to the hospital. I got five stitches of black thread. The nurse said it was going to be sore, but it wasn't.

That night I dreamt that I was round in the quarry and I was floating like God over the horns, bones and old cars. I wasn't wearing robes or anything – just shorts and a t-shirt. I was floating along and everyone was walking beside me. I was happy and so were they, especially our Patrick and Michael and Terry. They didn't chase me away. They loved me. I also had another dream that I was standing in a queue at the top of the class. Mrs Radcliffe was there and she was being strict as usual. I wore nothing but a vest, which was all yellow from pee. I had no underpants on. All the other boys had their clothes on. They didn't seem to notice. That was the dream.

* * *

Paddy Stewart took me, Patrick and Paul up the town to see Lundy. We walked up Bishop Street in our coats and wearing hats with floppy ears as it was freezing cold. We climbed up the narrow steps onto the city walls and, linking hands with each other in case we got lost, waded into a throng of men to find ourselves among a sea of grey, dull-green and black over-coats. The men were wearing flat caps and nearly everyone was smoking.

'Lundy is the tall man up there on the wall,' explained Paddy Stewart.

We couldn't see, so he lifted Patrick up first.

'D'ye see him, Patrick – the big, tall man up there?' he asked.

'Aye, I can see him. There he is up there!' replied Patrick, happy at the discovery.

'Right, Tony, up ye git!' Paddy Stewart said as he heaved me up in front of him over the standing crowd. 'D'ye see him?'

My eyes scanned the top of the crowd for the tallest man. A few stood out a foot or two taller than the rest.

'Aye, I see him over there,' I said, pointing in the wrong direction.

'Naw, not that way, Tony. Over there!' he said, turning me in the right direction.

'Oh aye, I see him now!' I said, pretending, not wanting to be left out, and he put me back on my feet.

'Right, wee Paul. C'mon, you now!'

He lifted Paul up to see and sure enough Paul said, 'Aye, Paddy. There's Lundy over there,' and he pointed in the right direction.

'Good boy yerself!' said Paddy Stewart, lowering him to our level.

'What's going to happen now, Paddy?' I asked.

'Oh, they're going to set Lundy on fire. They do it every year.'

God, I thought, *they're goin' to burn the tall man I saw in the crowd a minute ago!*

It wasn't until they set fire to a brightly painted twenty-foot dummy dressed like a pirate and attached to a scaffold, which I couldn't see, that I realised what he was talking about. Paddy held us up again one by one to get a good view of the burning of Lundy. Whoever Lundy was.[1]

* * *

---

1   Robert Lundy was governor of Derry during the siege of 1688–9. He was branded a traitor for promising to surrender the city to the army of King James.

Our Patrick was different from me and Paul. He didn't play football, his voice was different from ours, and he played with girls too much. I was out in the hall doing nothing and heard me ma and da talking in the scullery.

'Why do ye think our Patrick talks like that, d'ye know …?' me da asked her.

'Ach, it's just that he is always pallin' about wi' our Karen all the time,' me ma said.

Me da didn't say anything back – nothing that I could hear anyway. I wondered. I already knew that our Patrick was different.

* * *

Barry and Paddy McCool lived at the top end of our street on our side. Me ma said that Barry had been a jockey in England when he was younger. They had a stable at the side of the house where the huge white horse called Peggy lived.

One day me and our Paul were out in the street playing races. Barry was cleaning out the stable, saw us and called us in. Peggy the horse was in the stable and she was enormous.

'Do you want up on her back, Tony?' asked Barry.

'Aye, I'll go up,' I replied.

Paul said nothing but kept back. Barry stood me up on a stool; he got on a stool as well.

'Up you get,' he said as he lifted me under the arms and set me down on the horse's back.

The horse snorted and turned its head to see who was on her back. Seeing it was me, she turned away again. Barry lifted me down again.

'Paul, do you want up on Peggy?' Barry asked.

'Naw, I don't want to,' said Paul.

We raced back to the house to tell our ma and da.

'Mammy, our Tony was up on Peggy the horse's back there now,' said Paul with excitement in his voice. You would think it had been him who got up on the horse.

'God, isn't that great! Our Tony on the back of a big horse,' said me ma.

'McCools was an IRA house,' said Paddy Stewart to me ma one day in the scullery. 'The B-men were never out of it, raiding it. Years ago. They held an informer – a stooley – there one day in the stable. The whole street knew.' He giggled. 'God, they gave him a wild hard time. You could hear the roars of them at the bottom of the street. Aye, boys-a-boys.'

All new words to me. B-men. IRA. Informer. I knew nothing of what they were.

* * *

There was a cliff-edge to the quarry with a wire fence at the top to stop people falling over. As it came around towards our street it was very steep, but you could walk up it. We slid down it on car bonnets recovered from the quarry, like sleighs on the snow. We never had snow sleighs. Car bonnets were very heavy so the bigger boys – Davy McKinney and Davy and Tommy Barbour – would work together to carry the bonnet up the slope to the top. At the top we all jumped on. If there were too many it couldn't be pushed to get going, so a few of the smaller boys were rolled off. With a good push the bonnet would take off down the slope and come to a stop where the slope levelled at the bottom. One time Jacqueline McKinney jammed her leg underneath as it was moving down the slope. Her leg was cut, and away she went home, crying her eyes out. A few minutes later she came back for more. The bonnet went like mad down the slope when the grass was wet.

We fought with the Bishies over who owned the bankin'. We had stoning wars with them. The Bishies were from Bishop Street. Sean and Seamus Donnelly were fearless Bishie warriors with a deadly aim. They were better than us and had the height of the bankin' in their favour. Moore Street and Hamilton Street were at the bottom. This was no good. We played football with the Bishies, too, on the bankin'. At the end there was always a stoning war. Boys got split with stones. The Bishies chased us down the bankin'.

One day I was trapped at the bottom of the quarry and Seamus Donnelly was at the top. He was in the same year as me at school. I had nowhere to hide. I was good at throwing stones and threw some at him, but he had the height of the quarry for protection. I ducked down behind an old car for cover as the stones sparked off the rusty metal.

A stone whacked me on the top of my head. The car was useless. My head felt sore and I could feel blood with my fingers. I didn't cry. I ran to the bottom of the cliff and hid in tight to the face. He was pelting away – just me and him. Another stone hit me on the forehead. The blood ran down into my eyes. I was crying now, but he didn't stop – it made him worse and he laughed as he threw. I made a bolt for it, zigzagging across the open ground the way the US Marines did, until I reached the safety of the rear of Moore Street where the McCools lived. I looked back through the blood and the tears to the top of the quarry, and Seamus Donnelly was gone.

'Jesus, Mary and Saint Joseph,' me ma shouted as I came through the back door.

'What were you doing, ye stupid eejit ye?' said me da as he yanked me by the arm, a bottle of Doby washing-up liquid in his other hand, towards the door to the yard.

He bent me down under the tap, turned the water on over my head and washed the cuts with the Doby. The cold water stung the open wounds, but I kept still as he did his work. Me ma stood at the back door giving off about the savages up the bankin' and saying that I wasn't to play up there any more.

'Them cuts'll need a stitch,' said me da, inspecting the damage.

'I think you're right, Paddy,' said me ma.

As on the day I cut my hand, me ma wrapped strips of cut-up pillowcase around my gashed head and we got the usual two buses to the hospital at Altnagelvin. The nurse gave me an injection in the arm. I didn't cry or pull back. The doctor started sewing my head back together with stitches, warning me that it would be sore. It was. I got eleven stitches, I told the boys that evening in the street: five in the back and six on the front.

'Me ma said the Bishies are savages and I'm not allowed up the bankin' any more,' I added.

'That's just stupid,' said Michael McKinney. 'Sure we own the bankin'.'

'What happened you, Tony Doherty? What the hell were you up to up that bankin'?'

The voice belonged to Nan McGowan who lived in No. 8. She was standing at her door. Nan had a normal leg and another that was twice as broad at the calf and had a huge brown mark on it that looked like a misshaped pancake. Her dark skirt came to just below the knee. She lived with her sister, Mary Jane, who was shorter and had two normal legs.

'He got split by the Bishies,' said Dooter McKinney.

'Aye, I got split twice, so I did,' I told her. 'Me ma said the Bishies are savages.'

'And so they are. They're nothing but animals,' said Nan and she reached into her apron and brought out her purse. 'Go and get yourself some swiddies in the shop.' She gave me a shilling.

Paddy McKinney came out of his house, shouting. He

lived across the street from us. He had a pot on his head and was carrying a yard brush with a bread knife tied to the end. He was shouting and roaring – not words, just shouting and roaring. Me ma said he was suffering from shell-shock from the war. He had a suit on and wore shiny black shoes. He ran from the bottom of the street to the top, turned at McCools' and ran back down again. He roared at the top of his voice. He always did this. This is what he did in the street. The street was full of children.

'Poor critter,' said Nan at her door as Paddy shot past with his knife and brush. 'What a waste of a good man.'

Me ma said one day that Nan and Mary Jane were two old maids in the garret. I didn't know what she meant.

We went to the shop.

Once during a war with the Bishies, I threw a stone and it collided mid-air with a stone fired in our direction. You could hear the sharp crack, like a shot, of stone on stone. Both stones dropped to the ground with a clump. Dooter McKinney saw it and told everyone. I was some shot, a force to be reckoned with.

* * *

The Americans were sending a rocket to the moon. Me and Dooter and our Paul went up the bankin' to get a better look. We lay flat on the grass looking up at the blue, cloudless sky. Dooter was in the middle.

'You have to look really hard. The rocket'll be tiny,' I said.

That's what the boys were saying at school. They knew. We stayed on our backs and looked. It was a very warm day. The grass was dry and warm.

'There it is!' shouted our Paul.

'Where? Where?' shouted me and Dooter.

'There! Look!' He pointed up into the blue sky.

I jumped over Dooter and Paul to get to the other side to see better. We followed the general direction of his finger and, sure enough, there it was. A tiny silver pin in the cloudless blue sky. It was hardly moving but it was there. We could see it!

* * *

Chalk The Water lived in Hamilton Street, near Paddy Melaugh's shop. He had a donkey and cart. Children in the street called out 'Chalk The Water!' as he rode past on his donkey and cart. He would shout something back and wave his stick.

'Me da said Chalk The Water's not the full shilling,' Terry McKinney once told us. Terry knew everything. He knew all the rules of football. When I won the ball off him, one day when we were playing out at the Daisyfield, he said, 'You robbed me, so you did. It's a free kick to us.' Robbing sounded like a foul so he got his free kick. I knew I won the ball fairly, but he knew everything.

Me and Dooter were in Chalk The Water's back yard. We just knocked and his ma let us in through the house.

'Can we go out wi' ye the day?' we asked. We never called him Chalk The Water, but he didn't have any other name.

He mumbled something back in agreement from under his flat cap, which was too big for his head. His eyes were deep-set in his thin face under the shadow of his cap, which he always fidgeted with, turning it this way and that. We understood. We helped him attach the cart to the donkey. The cart was painted red. We patted the donkey as he attached the bridle through its yellowy teeth. Up we got, sitting one on each side. Chalk The Water's ma came out to open the gates to the lane and gave him an old, worn canvas bag. Inside there'd be a packet of Custard Creams and a bottle of milk. He mumbled something back to her. *Thanks, Mammy*, we understood.

We were moving. We were going to the dump out at Prehen – at least we thought it was a dump. That's where Chalk The Water always went. As we rode down Hamilton Street, some children and adults shouted up at him, 'Chalk The Water!' and he shouted something back and waved his stick. He held the reins with his other hand. We waved down at them as we clattered noisily past. At the end of the street we turned left onto the Foyle Road towards the lower deck of Craigavon Bridge. The noise of the donkey's clip-clopping hooves echoed loudly between the two decks as we crossed

43

over to the Waterside and went straight out the road towards Prehen. No one shouted on the Waterside.

When we reached Prehen, Chalk The Water turned off the road into the dump. He got off the cart and so did we. He mumbled something. *I'm going away and will be back in a minute*, we understood. He went away. We patted the donkey's nose and ears.

'Chalk The Water's real name is Benedict,' said Dooter.

'How d'ye know?' I asked.

'Our Terry told me,' he said.

It must be true then, I thought. Chalk The Water came back after a few minutes.

'Are we getting the Custard Creams now, Benedict?' asked Dooter.

Chalk The Water looked at him, an expression of doubt in his deep-set eyes, and he mumbled something. *You don't call me Benedict*, we understood. Chalk The Water lifted the canvas bag from the cart, opened the Custard Creams and gave us three each. He opened the bottle of milk, took a mouthful and handed it to me. I drank some milk and handed it to Dooter. He drank and gave it back to Chalk The Water.

Chalk The Water mumbled something about the Custard Creams. *I love Custard Creams*, we understood.

'We love Custard Creams as well, so we do,' we said.

Chalk The Water looked across the river and mumbled something we didn't understand. He mumbled again and pointed over towards our street across the river. We understood.

'Is that our street there?' I asked, pointing across the river.

'Aye,' said Chalk The Water. We understood.

It was a nice day but it started to mizzle. We got down and sat underneath the cart until it passed. Chalk The Water got up, mumbled something and made a gesture towards the gate of the compound. *Time to go home*, we understood.

* * *

A few days later Chalk The Water was coming down Hamilton Street on the donkey and cart. We were playing tig beside the cottages up the lane.

'Chalk The Water!' we all shouted as he went past. 'Chalk The Water!'

Chalk The Water shouted something back and waved his stick at us. He clip-clopped on down the street towards Foyle Road and turned left towards the bridge. We went back to our tig.

* * *

One warm, sunny day, me da took us out to the yard and me ma came out after us with our Patrick. She was wearing a green and yellow dress with shapes on it that looked like wonky eyes. She looked nice. Her dark hair was down to her waist and was parted in the middle. We were lined up against the wall – Karen, me and our Paul.

'Patrick got a new camera and wants to take a photo of yis,' said me ma.

Me da stood in the line as well.

'Right, yous are looking great,' said me ma. 'Now everyone, smile and say "cheeeeese".'

We smiled and said 'cheeeeese'. Patrick held the camera up to his eye and pressed on the button. Instead of a click Karen got a squirt in the face. Before we caught on, both me and Paul got squirted in the face as well. He was a good shot. We all laughed. We couldn't believe that they could make a water-pistol out of a camera. We all got turns squirting at the line-up. It was only fair.

* * *

Me da sang 'The Black Velvet Band' to me ma when he had beer in him. He sang it in me granny's house at Christmas when everyone came, drank beer and had a party. We were allowed to stay at the top of the stairs and only came down to the sitting-room door when someone started singing. The bottled beer and lemonade were stacked in wooden crates beside the front door where they were delivered a few days before Christmas on an Iriscot's lorry. Me aunt Lorraine was allowed to bring in bottles of Carling Black Label to the sitting room where everyone was, but was chased out again. After the song was over we were chased back up to the top of the stairs. 'The Black Velvet Band' was about me ma because her eyes shone like diamonds and she tied her hair up with her black velvet band. She sat on me da's knee and looked into his face as he sang. She had long hair like Cher, parted in the middle but with a fringe at the front. So did our Karen. But the song was about me ma.

2

PATSY, EILEEN AND FAMILY

My da and ma, Patsy Doherty and Eileen Quigley, first made direct eye contact across the high-backed booths of Macari's Italian Ice-Cream Parlour on William Street, where my uncle Eugene worked part-time. It turned out that Patsy already had an eye for her: she had passed him and his mucker Johnny McFadden in the Guildhall Square one day and he had said to Johnny, 'D'ye see that girl Quigley over there with the ponytail and the tanned feet? I'm goin' to marry her!' Johnny told me da later that he thought he was nuts.

As Eileen was leaving Macari's with her friend, Iris Quigley (no relation), Patsy and Johnny, both Teddy boys in full battle dress, including the blue suede shoes and coiffed and lacquered hair, blocked the door while Patsy asked could he walk her home. She agreed and they headed up Rossville Street, with friends in tow, towards the Brandywell, where they both lived.

When they had reached the end of Moore Street, Patsy asked her for a date and she agreed. Several nights later they met for the date. Patsy showed up at the front door of No. 6 Moore Street with a box of Milk Tray and a twenty-pack of

Sweet Afton cigarettes for Eileen, as was the custom at the time. However it happened, they ended up having a row on their first date and Patsy concluded the encounter by throwing the box of chocolates into Meenan's Field beside the Gasyard. Eileen kept the fancy fags secure in her handbag.

Their next encounter was also somewhat unfortunate. Eileen and a group of her friends were making their way to the Crit – the Criterion Ballroom on Foyle Street – when they passed the hapless Patsy Doherty and Johnny McFadden tapping people for money to get into the dance hall. Eileen was mortified with embarrassment for, despite losing the luxury of the Milk Tray chocolates, she still considered the raven-haired Patsy her boyfriend.

* * *

The Doherty family of Paddy and Cassie lived in the prefabs in Anne Street in the Brandywell. The prefabs were houses made mostly of corrugated tin, probably with a high dose of asbestos, and erected in large prefabricated sections. They were like ovens in the summer and fridges in the winter, me da told us. Paddy and Cassie had three daughters: Maureen, Margaret and Kathleen (Kay), and two sons: Joe and Patsy, also called Paddy or 'the Skelper' by some of his friends. He was born in September 1939 at 281 Lecky Road in the Brandywell. His full name was Patrick Joseph Doherty, which is strange, because his brother was named Joseph too.

In Ireland, especially the north, we tend to regard ourselves as being from one community of people or another and that was the way it's always been – a form of pure-blood thinking. The reality is very different, as I was to find out later in life. My granny Cassie's father was from a Presbyterian family, the McFredericks, from out the road in Killea, but he married a Catholic and turned Catholic himself. His name was Joseph McFrederick and he was killed in 1917 while serving with the Royal Irish Rifles during the First World War in Flanders Field in Belgium. While he left six daughters, including Kathleen (Cassie), and one son, sadly the McFrederick name in both Killea and Derry is no more.

Given that my granny Doherty was, therefore, half-Protestant, that made my daddy, Patsy, a quarter Protestant and me an eighth Protestant at least, since it turns out my mother's family also had Presbyterian blood in their veins. One day in the early 1990s, a Lollipop Man stopped me in a local café and told me the story of our families' history. He knew me but I didn't know him. We were distant cousins. The story goes that, after the famine in the 1840s, two sisters by the surname of Taggart walked from Ramelton, a small town on the Fanad Peninsula in County Donegal, to Derry in search of work. They settled in Derry, eventually marrying two brothers from St Columb's Wells by the name of Quigley. My granda Connor Quigley was a grandson of one of the Taggart sisters. The Lollipop Man was a grandson of the other sister.

My granny Sally Quigley's maiden name was McLaughlin, as common as Doherty in Derry and neighbouring Inishowen. Her father was a trade union activist, an avowed communist who wasn't fond, to put it mildly, of the Catholic Church that dominated most aspects of life and set the moral standards for the Catholic population in those days. In the late 1950s, after Sally and Connor had moved to the new Creggan Estate, she was mortified when the priest read the names of known communists from the altar, my great-granda's name prominent among them, condemning them for their godless beliefs. Of course, he wasn't there to hear for himself; Granny Sally told me that no one ever had the nerve to tell him of the public condemnation. 'He would have went to the priest's door and raised a row,' she said with a laugh.

In the 1950s my grandparents were part of the migration of largely Catholic families who moved from the area known nowadays as the Bogside, as well as from St Columb's Wells, Springtown Camp and other rundown slum-type houses, to the brand new housing project of the Creggan Estate, up the hill and surrounding the city cemetery on three sides.

At the top end of Central Drive, heading towards the Creggan Reservoir and Holywell Hill, was the ráth, known locally as 'the Cropie'. It's a large, circular site that probably was a place of some political importance before English came into use. It was said to have become a base for the French artillery under King James to fire cannon in the direction of the city walls during the siege of the city in 1690. I have no memory of the Cropie before we moved from Creggan, but it was later to become an important place for me when we were evacuated at the start of the Troubles.

Sally's mother, my great-granny, was involved with the Irish Volunteers in Derry between 1914 and 1922, a period of political and military tumult. There are stories of her marching with her comrades on the road between Derry and Carrigans in Donegal at that time. I didn't get to know her very well. My memories of her are simply of an old woman dressed in black who walked with a slight limp. She died in 1976 and she was waked in me granny and granda's new house in Mulroy Gardens, Creggan, one street up the hill from Central Drive, where I was born. By then most of their family had married and left and they needed a new house for a smaller family.

I was in my early teens by then. I came home from school for lunch and me great-granny's remains were being waked in the small dining room beside the kitchen at the rear of the house. Her sallow face could be seen from the kitchen where me granny was making lunch. I looked into the room several times to see if there was any movement from great-granny's hands or face. We went into the sitting room and ate our lunch with the TV on. Granny Sally drifted off to sleep after she smoked an Embassy Red. I was dying for a fag as well, but her handbag was closed and sitting at her feet on the floor. I'd remembered seeing two saucers full of fags sitting on a low wooden coffee table in the middle of the dining room where the coffin was. I got up quietly from the chair so as not to wake Sally up and went to the door of the dining room.

I was about to walk in to lift a fag and a few more for later when my eyes were drawn to the face in the coffin. I instantly lost the nerve to steal the cigarettes with her able to watch me. So I got down on my hands and knees at the doorway and looked up to see what I could see of her face. All I could see was the tip of her sharp nose above the padded rim of the coffin. Reassured that I was now out of view, I slowly crept the short distance from the door to the coffee table and reached out to lift a handful of fags. Just then, a low voice said, 'The Good Lord is watching you.' My hand hung motionless over the fags and I swear my heart stopped altogether. *Jesus Christ, she's alive!* I thought, my hand frozen in mid-steal. *What the fuck am I goney do?*

There followed a few seconds of excruciating silence as I was effectively trapped by the voice of an old woman supposed to be dead in her coffin. My eyes were drawn back up towards it. There was no change. The sharp tip of her nose was still all there was to be seen of her. *Maybe I'm hearing things*, I thought, and contemplated having another go at a few free smokes. 'The Good Lord is watching you, boy,' said the voice again, this time louder and from behind me.

I turned my head slowly to see who owned the voice,

expecting to see my great-granny's ghost bearing down on me. Instead, I saw my granny Sally standing in the kitchen with me in full view, my hand still hovering above the saucer of fags.

Needless to say, my walk back to St Joseph's Secondary School was all the lonelier without the smoke.

Sally's birth name was Sarah, but, once married, she was commonly known as Sally. Granda Connor's real name, on the other hand, was Patrick. My mother, Eileen Teresa Quigley, was the eldest daughter of Connor and Sally Quigley, and was born in April 1942.

Granny and Granda Quigley had a large enough family, as well as a few stillborns. Along with me ma there were Anna, Eugene, Seamus, Patsy, Celine, John, Mary, Michael, Gerard (known as Jerrit), Siobhán and Joseph, with Lorraine at the tail end. While Lorraine was officially my aunt, she was nearly three years younger than me; such were the times without either contraception or the Pope's blessing.

* * *

Despite their disappointing first two encounters, Patsy Doherty and Eileen Quigley continued to date. Eileen was a very beautiful young woman and Patsy was considered to be a great catch. Word has it that they were the glamorous couple of the late 1950s in working-class Derry – a version of Posh and Becks without the money ... or the legs: Eileen was five foot two, while Patsy towered over her at five foot four. Patsy and Granda Connor got on great together as Patsy was polite, charming and, of course, enjoyed the beer and the craic.

While Patsy and Eileen were still dating, Eileen became ill. Granny Sally was suspicious and took her to the doctor, who confirmed that her daughter was expecting a baby, their first grandchild. Sally and Connor were heartbroken and despondent at first, because children conceived or born out of wedlock were considered shameful and socially embarrassing, and they had better expectations of Eileen, their eldest.

However, as was the done thing at the time, Patsy Doherty and Eileen Quigley were quickly married in St Mary's Chapel, Creggan, on 18 April 1960, an Easter Monday morning, just two days after Eileen had turned seventeen. After the 8 a.m. mass the eighty or so guests were treated to a wedding breakfast at 26 Central Drive. Food was served on borrowed trestle-tables covered with fresh white cloths. Eileen's sister Anna was the bridesmaid, while her other sisters, Celine and Mary, helped to serve the breakfast. The newly-weds spent their honeymoon in Belfast, where they stayed in a guest house in the Ardoyne.

At the end of October 1960, Karen Doherty was born at 26 Central Drive (Granny Sally was also pregnant at the time with my uncle Joe). In late February 1961, Patrick Joseph Doherty came into the world, and almost two years later, on 1 January 1963, I was born: Anthony Christopher, the second-last of the Doherty wains to be born at Central Drive. Me ma tells me that the name Anthony came to me da after he saw the face of St Anthony at a window of a house he was walking past on Lecky Road. After going back again to check, the face was still at the window and he considered this as a sign from God. The name Christopher, another saint, was thrown in for good measure.

In the early 1960s me da worked for long periods as a labourer in England because work was scarce in Derry. He came back for a long period when me ma had a threatened miscarriage with Paul in November 1963. He wrote and sent money to me ma and phoned her once a week at the red phone box on the Foyle Road. His letters, written in blue ink on the broad-lined pages of a small, pale-blue writing pad, which survived in a Quality Street tin until the 1980s, spoke of his longing to see his three children soon. 'How's wee curly Tony doing?' he asked in one of them.

The first four of the Doherty children were born into the Quigley household of 26 Central Drive, Creggan. Central Drive, by the standards of housing in the 1960s, was as close to luxury as you could get. The house had four bedrooms, an indoor toilet and bathroom, a large scullery kitchen and a sizeable living room. It also had a steep, sloping garden at the front with a picket fence and a large, long rectangle of a garden at the rear that backed onto Dunree Gardens.

However, by the time my younger brother, Paul, arrived

on 1 February 1964, 'premature and looking like a Christmas turkey on the corridor floor of Altnagelvin Hospital' my mother said, space in the luxury house was becoming a problem. Granny Sally had twelve children of her own (though some had left home by 1964), and her house was bursting at the seams with wains, teenagers and young adults. It's not hard to work out the maths and the square footage per head. Something had to give.

In the spring of 1964 we moved to 6 Moore Street in the Brandywell, in the south of the city near the river. The house in Moore Street had been in the family's possession in some form or other since the 1940s. It wasn't just a physical move; it was also a move back in time out of the modern, spacious house in Central Drive into a nineteenth-century two-up-two-down terraced house with an outside toilet in a white-painted stone and mortar back yard. Where Central Drive had been bedecked with the furniture, fixtures, gadgetry and trappings of the fifties and sixties, 6 Moore Street was straight out of the sepia-toned twenties and thirties with its coal or block-fired range cooker, a chaise longue, which became an entertainment centre for us children, and the blue-and-white china dogs sitting in watch on either side of the ancient clock.

At one end of the street was Foyle Road, which led on to Letterkenny Road out to the Killea border with Donegal. Beyond Foyle Road was the wide river bank and the 'Line', the route of the old railway that used to shuttle passengers to and from the western seaboard of Donegal. The railway track was long gone by my childhood days, but it was still referred to as 'out the Line'. The only buildings out the Line were three air-raid shelters left over from the Second World War.

As it turned out, an old relative of me granny Sally's, Paddy Stewart, came with the house. We called him Uncle Paddy, but we knew he wasn't an uncle. Paddy was a lovable old man, rotund, red-nosed and always wore a suit, black shiny shoes, a greatcoat, or Walyee coat as it was called then, and, of course, his flat cap. It was said that he used to play for Derry City FC in the 1930s along with his brother Gerry – an idea that enthralled us, given that we lived near the Brandywell Football Stadium. It was also said that the two brothers worked in the pottery factories of Stoke-on-Trent for most of their lives between bouts of unemployment in Derry.

Paddy Stewart (we always gave him his full title) drank his stout in the Silver Dog and Mailey's Bar, and was even more lovable and red-nosed when he came home half-cut or drunk. He was very independent – he cooked and cleaned, and lodged in one room at the back of No. 6. When both me ma and da were working, Paddy would have our dinner ready on the range when we came in from school.

While Paddy Stewart occupied the small back bedroom, the six of us Dohertys slept in the larger front bedroom overlooking the street. Four children slept in one bed, head to toe, and me ma and da were in the other, though Paul spent his first year or two in a drawer up on two chairs beside their bed, as was the custom.

Me da drank stout too, but he was also partial to a Carling Black Label on occasion. Whiskey was like firewater to him, after which a nark or a row would be likely. Luckily for his friends and family he didn't drink it often. He was prone to spending a fair bit of time in the Silver Dog and me ma would dispatch me to the bar to tell him he had a family living up the street! Initially, I felt a bit odd being sent to deliver this message, but the financial rewards from me da's friends in the bar soon helped me to get over any awkwardness.

3

MOORE STREET DOWNFALL

At school we were learning to do sums and read books. I loved reading, writing and spelling. I was good at them but I wasn't fussed on the sums. Mrs Radcliffe held a competition to see who was the best speller in the class. There was a special prize for the winner but nobody knew what it was. She called out a word and you wrote it down with your pencil at the top of a new page on your jotter so she could see it spelt right or wrong as she walked up and down between the rows of wooden desks.

'All right, children. Are you ready?' she called out to start after we came in from the yard when dinnertime was over.

'Yes, Mrs Radcliffe!' we called back, more or less simultaneously.

'Write down at the top of your clean pages the word "chair",' she said.

The room fell silent except for the sound of thirty boys thinking and scribbling with their sharpened pencils. I wrote down CHAIR on my jotter, checked it again and sat watching Mrs Radcliffe, who stood beside the blackboard at the top of the class. 'Everybody finished writing the word "chair"?' she asked and the class responded with a 'Yes, Mrs Radcliffe.' Mrs Radcliffe took off on her journey in her flat, black slip-on shoes, walking between the rows of desks, checking each jotter as she passed, turning over the jotter of each word 'chair' spelt wrongly as she went, and leaving the correctly spelt ones as they were.

'Those who got it wrong, put your pencils down,' she instructed and about half the class put their pencils down. She then proceeded to write the word 'chair' on the blackboard. Mrs Radcliffe always used really squeaky chalk and the word 'chair' squeaked loudly in the quiet classroom as she wrote each letter down. The squeaking chalk hurt your teeth.

'Right, the rest of you write down the word "knife",' and again there was silence except for fewer pencils scribbling on the jotters. I wrote down the word KNIFE in my jotter.

After a few seconds, Mrs Radcliffe said, 'All finished writing the word "knife"?' and we all said, 'Yes, Mrs Radcliffe.' She took off again, this time only checking the desks with open jotters and turning the wrong spellings over as before. Back she went to the top of the class and squeaked out the word 'knife' under the word 'chair'. About eight of the class, me included, had their jotters facing up the right way in front of them.

'All right now, please write down the word "apple",' and the eight or so boys still in the competition began to write the word down. I wrote down the word APPLE in my jotter.

'All finished?' she asked, and again took off on her journey and by the time she returned to the blackboard, only me and Ciarán McLaughlin had our jotters facing up the right way on our desks. Ciarán wore glasses and was from Abercorn Road. Two others in the class wore glasses as well: Damien Healey and Damien Harkin, both from the Bog. Mrs Radcliffe squeakily wrote down the word 'apple' under the other two words on the blackboard.

'Tony Doherty and Ciarán McLaughlin,' said Mrs Radcliffe, 'well done the both of you!' She paused, thinking. 'And now we'll see who the best speller in the class is. Write down the word "blackboard".' *That's easy*, I thought, *sure it's only two words, black and board put together.* I wrote down the word BLACKBOARD in my jotter and so did Ciarán McLaughlin. Mrs Radcliffe came round, looked at the two words written down in the jotters and said 'Well done' again as she went back to the blackboard and proceeded to write the word 'blackboard' in squeaky white letters below the word 'apple' and the others.

'Right,' she said turning round again, 'write down the word aer-o-plane,' pronouncing the O to break up the word. I had never written the word aeroplane before, but I had seen it written down somewhere and knew that it didn't start with AIR, but AER. I wrote down the word AEROPLANE in my jotter, the way I thought correct from memory.

Mrs Radcliffe came down from the top of the class again

and looked at the two jotters. Both of us had got it right again. 'Well done, Tony and Ciarán,' she said, almost with a smile, and she turned and walked back to write the word 'aeroplane' under the growing list of words on the blackboard. When she turned round again she said, 'Both Tony Doherty and Ciarán McLaughlin are joint winners of the spelling competition and will get their special prize before they go home today.'

As three o'clock approached, the whole class had their eyes on Mrs Radcliffe to see from where the prizes were going to come. There was no sign of an obvious prize anywhere. When the bell eventually rang, Mrs Radcliffe lifted her shiny black handbag from under her table and took out her purse. Even though the bell had gone no one was allowed to move in Mrs Radcliffe's class until she said so. That was the rule. Everyone sat and watched her opening her purse and, when she closed it, you could hear coins rattling in her hand. 'Tony Doherty and Ciarán McLaughlin, can you come up here, please?' she said, and both of us went up to the front beside her table. 'Here you are, one for you and one for you,' she said as she pressed a shilling coin in our hands, 'and congratulations. Give Tony and Ciarán a round of applause, boys,' and the whole class clapped.

When I got outside, Karen and Patrick were waiting for me. 'What was all that clapping about?' asked Karen.

'I won a shilling for me spelling,' I said, holding the shilling out for them to see.

'A whole shilling! God, that Mrs Radcliffe must be rich!' said Karen.

'Can we go to Wee Johnny's for something?' I asked my older sister.

'Aye, surely,' she replied and we dandered out through the archway onto Bishop Street. Wee Johnny's shop was a house in a short terraced row just up from the archway on the same side of Bishop Street. When we went in the shop was full of wains all shouting their orders at the one time and holding pennies up for Wee Johnny. Wee Johnny repeated every order as he went.

'A bag of Tayto cheese 'n' onion, Johnny.'

'A bag of Tayto cheese 'n' onion, surely,' said Johnny, his hand out for the money first. 'Now, who's next?' he said, as if he had to ask.

'A bottle of cream soda and two Whoppers.'

'A bottle of cream soda and two Whoppers, surely,' he replied, with the hand out.

'Two treacle dainties and a Bubbly.'

'Two treacle dainties and a Bubbly, surely,' said Wee Johnny, taking the money and handing over the sweets.

It was my turn.

'A bottle of Sarsparilla and the rest in Fruit Salads and Black Jacks,' I said, holding the shilling up for him at the counter.

'A bottle of Sarsparilla and the rest in Fruit Salads and

Black Jacks, surely,' he repeated, taking the shilling coin off my hand. He lifted the wee bottle of Sarsparilla off the shelf behind him, opened it with the opener attached to the counter and handed it over. I grabbed the bottle and our Patrick took a handful of Fruit Salads and Black Jacks from him. As I turned to leave I noticed a huge bluebottle floating in the neck of the bottle of the Sarsparilla.

'Hi, Johnny,' I called out, 'there's a dirty big bluebottle in this bottle of Sarsparilla!' and held the bottle up for him. 'I want another wan.'

'A dirty big bluebottle in the bottle of Sarsparilla, another wan surely, son,' repeated Johnny and took the bottle from me. 'Here ye go,' he said as he handed me another one. We left the crowded shop and headed down Bishop Street towards home. As we walked down the hill towards the Brandywell we ate our way through the Black Jacks and the Fruit Salads. Black Jacks were small, black, liquorice-flavoured toffee sweets, and Fruit Salads were small pink and orange fruit-flavoured toffee sweets.

As I chewed happily on a mouthful of the Fruit Salads, I struggled to get control of the softening block in my mouth, and felt a sharp pain shoot up from my jaw to my eye. I let a yelp out of me and put my hand up to my mouth to soothe the pain.

'God, what the hell's that?' I asked. 'I've a wile sore pain in my mouth!' and started to cry with the pain.

'It must be a toothache,' Karen said, adding, 'everybody gets them.'

'God, it's really wile sore,' I cried, holding my mouth, while still trying to suck on the remains of the lump of Fruit Salads in my mouth.

'Me ma or da'll put something on it when they come home from work,' said Karen.

After an agonising hour on the chaise longue holding my sore mouth, me ma came in through the sitting room door.

'God, son, what happened ye?' she asked.

'I've got a toothache. I ate too many oul Fruit Salads and they made a hole in me tooth. It's wile sore, Ma. Is there anything you can put on it for me?'

'Aye. I'll get ye something. Houl on a minute,' and with that she went out the door. She came back a few minutes later with a wee brown bottle and cotton wool in her hands.

'Right, sit you back on the sofa so we can see,' she said, which I did.

'Put your head back a bit over the arm,' she said, which I did as well.

'Oh dear!' she said, as she dabbed at my gums with the cotton wool, 'we'll have to get you to the dentist. That'll need to come out.'

The pain eased as the smell of Clove Rock invaded my mouth.

'What'll need to come out, Ma?' I asked.

'That tooth. It'll need to come out. Here, houl you that up to your gum,' she said, giving me the clove-soaked cotton wool as she got up and went to the kitchen.

The next afternoon Mrs Radcliffe said to me that me ma was waiting for me in the corridor to take me to the dentist, and we walked from the school down to Riverview House, where the dentist was. We went to the same building where I'd had my hearing test, but went in through a different door. Another nurse wearing a navy-blue uniform came out to where we were waiting, spoke to me ma on her own and after a few minutes the nurse brought us into the dentist's room. The dentist was a young, short-haired man wearing a white coat.

'Hello, Tony,' he said. 'You're here to get a tooth out?'

'Aye,' I said, looking around me at the trays and tools and the dentist's chair.

'You eating too many sweeties?' he asked.

'Aye, them oul Fruit Salads,' I answered, wondering how he knew.

'Well, let's see. Up you get on my chair and put your head back,' said the dentist, as he moved over me.

'Open your mouth wide,' which I did, and he poked inside my mouth with a few metal tools, mmming and ahhing to himself.

Up he got, said a few things to the nurse that I couldn't hear, and then the nurse came towards me, still lying back on the dentist's chair.

'Well, Tony,' said the nurse, 'I'm just going to put this over your face and you have to breathe deeply for a few seconds. Okay?' she asked and I nodded back to her the best I could. She placed what looked like a black mask over my face. 'Now, breathe in Tony,' said the nurse, and I breathed the rust-smelling gas for a few seconds.

I woke up from my deep sleep and the nurse and me ma were smiling down at me as I lay still on the dentist's chair. They were saying 'Wake up, Tony' right into my face. I could hear myself babbling something back and me ma and the nurse went into fits of giggling as they lifted me, an arm each, from the chair. My tongue was dry in my mouth and the nurse, still giggling away, put a clear plastic glass of red coloured water up to my mouth and told me to take a sip and spit it out in the wee white bowl beside the chair. The inside of my mouth felt like somebody else's; I could nearly put my whole tongue in the crater left by my tooth. I got to my feet after a minute or so and me ma asked me was I okay to go. I said 'Aye' and we headed unsteadily towards the door and out into Riverview Park. As we walked through the park, I asked me ma why they were laughing at me in the dentist's.

'Aw, don't talk,' she laughed. 'You woke up ranting and raving "I'm not deef Ma, amn't I not?"'

* * *

Brian McCool lived round the corner in Townsend Street, one street up from Moore Street. He was a nephew of Barry and Paddy, who owned Peggy the horse. I went into their sitting room with him one Saturday morning and he went upstairs. His big brother, Jake, was sitting on one end of the sofa and another big brother, Alec (known as Elec), was at the other end. Jake was reading a paper.

'Sit you down over there on the chair,' said Mrs McCool, pointing to a chair opposite. She was in the kitchen making tea.

I sat down opposite the sofa with Brian's big brothers on it. There was a coffee table in between us with a plate of tarts on it – yellow and pink iced tarts. My eyes locked on them.

I saw Jake catching me gawking at the tarts and I looked away. He lifted the paper up in front of his face and Elec looked at him. They knew. I looked away to the kitchen, wondering what was keeping Brian. But the tarts drew me back; I couldn't help gawking. I heard a noise from behind the paper.

Elec looked over at Jake again and smiled, first at him and then at me.

'Do you want one?' he asked, nodding at the tarts.

'One what?' I replied. I could feel my cheeks redden.

'A tart,' he said. 'Do you want one?'

He looked over at Jake, still hidden behind the paper, which was shaking by now.

'Naw, I'm all right,' I lied, quickly glancing from Elec back to the tarts.

'Here, take a wee tart. D'ye want a yellow one?' He lifted the plate from the table and held it out towards me.

'Naw, I'm all right, Elec. We're goin' out, me and Brian. I'm just waiting on him.'

Jake brought the newspaper down. His face was red and he looked happy.

'Take a wee tart, Tony,' he said, 'there's too many for us.' He looked at the tarts and then looked at me to give me the go-ahead.

'Here's the tea, boys,' said Mrs McCool, coming in from the kitchen. 'D'ye want a wee tart, Tony?' she said as she placed the mugs in front of her big sons.

'Aye, okay,' I replied and looked at Jake and Elec before reaching for a pink one.

We all smiled at one another as we ate the tarts.

* * *

We were going to Mass on a Sunday morning. We were outside the house in our good clothes when me da came out last. Becky and Mary Gallagher, who lived in the last house at the top end of the street, opposite Barry and Paddy McCool, were coming out to go to Mass as well. You only ever saw them when they were going to Mass. We didn't know which of them was Becky and which was Mary, so we called them

Oul Doll and New Doll. Oul Doll was the tallest. Paddy Stewart said they were from out the road in Killea, but they lived in our street.

Out they came dressed in black shawls with black skirts and black boots. Oul Doll went first, up and out of Moore Street towards Hamilton Street. New Doll followed right behind her, keeping step with her sister. We were going in the same direction. We followed in silence at a safe distance. Patrick and Paul started giggling into their hands. Me da knew we were watching, but all he said was 'Cut that cackle'. The two women stopped at the Grotto, turned briefly to bless themselves in perfect sync, and continued on their journey, one behind the other, up towards Hogg's Folly to Mass in the Long Tower Chapel. We all blessed ourselves as we passed the Grotto.

As they entered the chapel they stopped to dip their hands for holy water. Oul Doll waited for New Doll to dip and the two of them blessed themselves in unison before going inside. At Mass we sat a few rows behind them. At Holy Communion they manoeuvred from the pew as one and walked up to the altar, Oul Doll first, with New Doll in tow. After Communion down they came, Oul Doll followed by New Doll.

* * *

Our Karen was a witch. Me da called her Biddy Top Boot. She was in the bath one Saturday night. Me da called us in to see her hair held up with shampoo and brought up to a sharp point like a witch's hat.

When her front teeth fell out me da sent her to the shop for two sachets of Supersoft shampoo. When she came back she told me da that the man in the shop didn't know what she was asking for.

'So what did you ask for?' he asked her.

'Two thatheys of thuperthoft thampoo,' she replied.

'Two what?' he asked.

'Two thatheys of thuperthoft thampoo,' she repeated.

'But I didn't send you for two thatheys of thuperthoft thampoo, I sent you for two sachets of Supersoft shampoo.' He was laughing now.

'He didn't underthtand what I was thaying,' she said, not sure what the laughing was about. 'I had to point them out on the thelf above hith head,' she added, holding the two sachets of Supersoft shampoo out in the palm of her hand.

Me da bawled with laughter. So did we. Karen laughed too. Me da loved Karen. You could tell.

* * *

Paul hated water, especially the bath. He spoiled it for me; I loved the warm water on my skin and making waves. Our bath was a long, grey, tin one that was kept on a hook on the wall in the yard and brought in on a Saturday night. Me ma and da had to drag Paul in from the street. He stayed calm when he came in and while he took his clothes off. But when it was time to get into the water he struggled, writhed and kicked for all he was worth. Me ma had him by the arms and me da by the feet. One foot was in and then it was out again; two feet in and then one out over the side. When he got wet they couldn't hold on to him and he escaped, ran out of the room, slipped on the oilcloth and slid down the hall on his bare arse. Me da had to run after him and slide him back again. Both me ma and da were in stitches laughing by this stage. Both of them were wringing wet. The oilcloth was covered in water. Paul was crying, but they got hold of him again and carried him to the bath where he was stood up straight and he let me ma wet him with a warm facecloth. When he turned around his arse and legs were black from the oilcloth and it ran down in streaks like watery liquorice. He calmed down, the tears stopped and eventually he got into the water and enjoyed the bath.

* * *

'Me da's friend was in our bedroom last night,' said Karen as we sat on the black plastic sofa and chairs. 'Yous were all sleeping.'

'Who?' asked Patrick.

'Toby,' she said. 'I was the only one awake and he came into the room and sat down on the edge of the bed. He had sweets with him. He gave me some and I ate them.'

'What kind of sweets did you get?' asked Patrick.

'Wine gums,' she said. 'I ate them but I didn't like him sitting there on the bed.'

'Why not?' asked Patrick.

'I don't know. Yous were all sleeping and I wanted yous to wake up but yous didn't,' she replied.

'What happened then?' asked Patrick.

'He left and went downstairs. He didn't go in to say churrio to me ma and da. He just went out the front door,' she said. 'When me ma and da came up to get into bed, I told them that Toby was in the room and that he'd sat down on the bed and gave me sweets.'

'What did me da say?' asked Patrick.

'He whispered something to me ma, then went downstairs again and out the front door. Me ma followed him down but didn't go out. Me ma told me this morning that me da went round to Toby's house, said to Toby's ma what he did, and took him out to the street and battered him with his fists.'

'He must've stole something on the way out,' said Patrick. 'That's why he battered him.'

* * *

Me ma and da brought a baby girl back from the hospital. She slept in our bedroom in a drawer balanced on two chairs from the scullery. There was seven of us now in the bedroom. When we woke in the morning we would crowd round the drawer to look to see if she was awake before we got dressed for school. Me ma said to give her some air, so we stood back to give her air and then crowded round again. The baby's name was Colleen.

The bedroom ceiling fell in when we were at school. You could see the attic when you looked up through the wooden beams. It was like a cave. The bedroom light looked odd as it dangled from a piece of bare wood in the attic. The ceiling didn't fall on Colleen; she was downstairs with me ma.

* * *

'Hi mister, d'ye call you John Hume?' I shouted from across the street to a dark-haired man in a suit as he passed by. We were playing tig on Hamilton Street near Paddy Melaugh's shop.

'Aye, that's right, son,' he called back, laughing.

'Are you getting us a new house?' I asked, following him as he walked along the street.

'Do they call you Doherty?'

'Aye.'

'Yous are getting a new house. I'm going up to see your mammy and daddy now. You live in number six?' he asked.

'Aye, wi' the green door,' I said, adding, 'Our ceiling fell in ye know?'

He laughed and said, 'I do. Your mammy told me all about it,' and headed to our door and knocked.

I went back to playing tig.

4

AN ARMY SANGAR ON HAMILTON STREET

We moved house when I was six. A procession of children, only some of them Dohertys, came down the lane from Moore Street to 15 Hamilton Street bearing boxes, lampshades and bundles of bedclothes. We were moving again. It didn't take long. Paddy Stewart wasn't coming with us to Hamilton Street. He wanted to stay where he was. To get more peace, me ma said. The new house was a dull cream colour with a dull brown door and dull brown windowsills. Coffee and cream, it was called.

We brought our black plastic sofa and beds. We got a new bed as well from me granny Sally's house. Me ma and da got their own bedroom. Colleen stayed in with them in her drawer. Me and Paul had a bed of our own, and Karen and Patrick had a bed of their own. But the four of us were still in the one room. Their bed was over near the brown-tiled fireplace with their headboard facing the door, and me and Paul's bed faced out the window towards the front street. Downstairs, there was a room beyond the scullery called the bathroom. It had a white bath in it and a toilet. We must've left the tin bath in Moore Street. We had a new front room with orange carpet and a long brown press with brass handles. A brown plastic farm-horse stood on the floor beside the fireplace.

Hamilton Street was much longer than Moore Street. It curved away towards Lecky Road and the Bogside at one end and met Foyle Road at the other end near the river. It was a terraced street too, with houses built at odd levels. Across the street from our house was a row of four smaller houses that were more like cottages. The McKinneys had moved to Hamilton Street before us. There were now two McKinney families in the same street, and three Brown families. The Barbours – Davy, Tommy, Johnny and Hughie – lived a few doors to our right beside Gutsy McGonagle and then the Starrs. Further up and across the street to the left were the O'Donnells, the Kellys and the two McKinney families. There was a huge swarm of wains.

A few days after we moved in we came home from school to find the house had been painted from top to bottom. We had another green door, and green windowsills, and green in a band at the bottom where the house met the street. The walls were cream-coloured. Our cream walls met a brown house on the right and a lilac house on the left, the paint touching in straight lines from the top of the house to the bottom. Our drainpipe was green too. It stood out from the other houses in the street, even when you stood away down the street and looked up. It was great to live in a house that stood out from the rest, I thought.

* * *

Me and Paul went up the town with Paddy Stewart. In the Diamond a statue of a soldier was killing someone on the ground with his rifle and bayonet. We stood in the crowd surrounded by men in their long, dull overcoats. There were women there too. Someone was shouting about houses and jobs but we couldn't see a thing. Everyone clapped the speaker. We were bored but well-behaved.

On our way home Paddy took us into Neilly Doherty's, the barber's at the top of Anne Street, for a haircut.

'Hello, Paddy, how's the form?' asked Neilly.

'Hello, Neilly. Grand. I brought the two boys in for a chop.'

'Sit yous down there,' Neilly said to us. 'There's a few comic-cuts there on the table.'

An old man of about Paddy Stewart's age was getting his white hair cut and was looking at us in the large mirror. Neilly stood behind him. All his haircutting tools were sitting on a silver tray attached to the back of the big red chair. I picked up the *Beano*, but Paul just sat looking around him, watching the old man getting his hair cut.

Neilly finished with him and brushed the hair from his neck.

'Right, who's first then?' he asked as the old man left the shop.

'Away you go, Tony. Show Paul how easy it is,' Paddy said.

I got up on the big red chair and Neilly pumped it higher with his foot. He placed a large grey cape around my neck and tied it at the back. I could see the street in the mirror, and Paddy and Paul as well. Paddy was reading the paper for the racing and Paul was just watching me. Neilly switched on the electric razor that went with a hum and he started humming to himself as well as he ploughed through my thick fair hair. The cuttings tumbled onto my shoulders and fell to the floor. He used scissors at the front and turned the chair around so that I was facing him. In no time at all I was cut down to size and Neilly was brushing the hair from my neck and face.

'D'ye want lacquer on it, son?' he asked, with the bottle in his hand about to shoot. I hated the lacquer but I said, 'Aye, all right then', and he sprayed it all over my newly cut hair and patted it down with his hand at the front.

'There you go. Is the wee man next, then?' asked Neilly.

'Aye. Away up you go now, wee Paul,' said Paddy.

'Naw, I don't wanny.'

'C'mon, wee Paul. Sure didn't Tony get his cut?'

Paddy took him gently by the hand and led him to the chair. Neilly put the grey cape over him and tied it behind his neck. But Paul had his head bent down to his chest and his eyes were closed. Neilly lifted his chin up, but down his head fell again when Neilly took his hand away. Neilly placed his hand under Paul's chin and lifted it up again, looking over at Paddy and me. Down it fell again. Neilly laughed and so did Paddy.

'Oh, boys-a-boys! If you don't lift your head,' said Paddy, 'he'll have to cut a baldy spot on the top of it like a monk.'

Paul opened one eye and looked over at me in the mirror, smiled and lifted his head up for Neilly. But as soon as Neilly started with the electric razor on his neck the tears came. He didn't cry out – just silent tears that kept coming until Neilly sprayed him with the lacquer bottle and patted his hair down at the front.

'What about you, Paddy? Are you havin' a chop the day?'

'Naw, Neilly,' said Paddy, handing him money. 'I'll be in next week.'

Away we went out the door.

'I'm headin' over here to the bookies,' Paddy said. 'D'yous want to go on home yourselves?'

Me and Paul headed over towards Hamilton Street. There were wains out playing everywhere. The two of us were spied from afar. We knew what was going to happen next and just had to accept it; we walked in silence down the street with our heads bowed.

The playing stopped.

'The Dohertys got their hair cut! The Dohertys got their hair cut!' they all chanted, girls and boys. It was terrible.

'Baldy balls, baldy balls!' they called out.

We just kept walking. Paul was crying with the shame of it. I didn't cry, but I wanted to.

'Baldy balls, baldy balls!' echoed down the street until we reached the house.

When we came back out to play football later on there was no mention of the haircut.

* * *

John lived across the street with his da. Our Patrick said he was a spastic. Patrick called everyone a spa but John definitely was one. He was tall and lanky with dirty fair hair and blue eyes. He was called Fuck-a-dee because that's all he said; some people called him Eff-a-dee because they didn't curse. Our Patrick didn't care about cursing – he called him Fuck-a-dee, but not in front of me ma or da, or Eff-a-dee's own da.

Eff-a-dee said 'Fuck-a-dee' with the heel of his hand stuck in his mouth. He slabbered a lot over his jumper. When he came out of his house, one of the cottages opposite our house, his da came out with him. He said 'Oh Jesus, Da' as well. Sort of. It sounded like 'Oh Jeedit, Da', but we knew what he meant. He didn't play with us, but he would sometimes come over near us, the heel of his hand in his mouth, saying 'Fuck-a-dee' and smiling at us.

Eff-a-dee came out of his house as we played football in the street. He was wearing baseball boots. His da followed to keep an eye on him and tell him to stop cursing. But Eff-a-dee just said 'Fuck-a-dee' back to him and gave him a breathy, grinning laugh through the heel of his hand. Eff-a-dee circled some of us and we stopped playing. It was hard to play when he was on the pitch along with his da, so we just stopped to let him walk around us. When his da got fed up he called him to come back in, saying that they had to get ready to go out. Eff-a-dee's da didn't look at us. He just looked at Eff-a-dee and only spoke to him.

'Oh Jeedit, Da,' said Eff-a-dee.

'Right, son. C'mon now, till we go,' said his da.

'Oh Jeedit, Da,' said Eff-a-dee, louder, walking around us.

By this time some of us were sitting on the edge of the footpath, watching. He didn't want to go in.

'Come on now, son,' said his da, walking towards him.

'Fuck-a-dee,' said Eff-a-dee excitedly, the heel of his hand in his mouth.

'Now, John, no cursing. That's not nice now,' said his da.

'Oh Jeedit, Da,' said Eff-a-dee, walking ahead of him towards their house.

'Good boy, John,' said his da.

'Fuck-a-dee,' said Eff-a-dee. He was standing on the road, near his front door.

His da took his hand to lead him in. 'Good boy, John.'

'Oh Jeedit, Da! Oh Jeedit, Da!' squealed Eff-a-dee, agitated and refusing to move.

'That's a boy. C'mon in now, John. Be a good boy,' said his da.

'Fuck-a-dee! Fuck-a-dee! Fuck-a-dee!' Eff-a-dee squealed again.

His da gently pulled him in through the front door and closed it behind them.

We returned to our football.

* * *

Me ma got a box of apples from Eddie McKevitt, the Fruit Man who brought fruit and nuts to our door every Hallowe'en. The box of apples smelled nice and appley and the smell filled the whole downstairs. She also bought a pallet of sugar somewhere and it was brought to our house as well. She came in a day or two later with a bundle of green-dyed sticks tied together with cord. Toffee apples! The smell of sugar melting in a big pot on the gas cooker filled the house. She cut a green stick in three, stuck a piece of green stick into an apple and rolled it around the inside edge of the pot filled with melted sugar. She let it drip for a moment into the pot and then she set it down on a tray covered with baking paper, which would eventually hold twelve, sixteen, twenty, upturned toffee-coated apples, depending on the size of the tray. Some trays were round – Carling Black Label trays from the Silver Dog bar. They only held six apples or so. The scullery windows were open and the trays were left on the table to let the toffee cool down and harden. The toffee formed a flat base on the tray as it hardened. Three shops sold them for her: Melaugh's shop, a shop in Bishop Street and a shop on the corner of Quarry Street. When we were sent to Melaugh's for a message, me ma's toffee apples were sitting on the counter beside the buns.

Karen and Patrick were allowed to go round the doors the whole way up Bishop Street to sell them from Colleen's pram. Me and Paul weren't allowed to sell them in case big boys took the money off us, but we followed at a distance from the pram until they got too far up Bishop Street. Big boys once took the pram off them, scooped out a handful of toffee apples for themselves and let the pram free-wheel down Stanley's Walk over in the Bog until it hit a car at the bottom. This was why the Bog was out of bounds for us, me ma said.

Gutsy McGonagle lived a few doors down the street with his ma and da. He had a cousin with red hair called Tony, who stayed with him all the time. Tony never talked and always looked like he wanted to cry or hit you. Gutsy's ma started making toffee apples as well. They were darker than ours.

'Me ma makes them with better sugar than yous,' said Gutsy.

Me ma was raging and gave off to me da. Me da didn't do anything. Gutsy and Tony went round the doors with a pram. Colleen's pram was better and newer-looking; shinier too.

'I looked into Gutsy's ma's kitchen window,' said our

Patrick. 'She was rolling the toffee apples in the po on the cooker. That's why they're dark brown.'

A po! That people pish in! Word got round the street. Gutsy's ma stopped making her toffee apples. No one would buy them off her.

* * *

Me ma was ironing in the sitting room. There was a smell of hot shirts. The clothes were hanging on hangers attached to the scullery door or folded neatly on the chair. The iron didn't look hot. It was pure shiny and upright on the ironing board. Me ma was in the scullery doing something else. I couldn't resist: I rested my right hand flat on the iron. The shock of the heat kicked me back. Too late! I couldn't shout or cry. I held my hand under my armpit to hide the pain. Me ma came back from the scullery.

'What's wrong wi' you?' she asked suspiciously.

'Nothin', Mammy. I'm going out.'

It was my own fault for being stupid. The iron put a sheen on my hand for weeks. And it was painful to make a fist.

* * *

The Barbours lived four doors down from us. The da was called Davey. He was a huge, strong-looking man. The ma was small and round and didn't speak much – at least, not in the street.

'Mr Barbour enjoys his pint,' me ma observed when he staggered past our house on his way home.

Johnny Barbour was the same age as me, Tommy Barbour was the same age as Patrick, Davey Barbour was the same age as Karen, and Hughey Barbour was the same age as our Paul. There were no girls. Johnny was my mucker, but so were Tommy and Davey. Davey was big and strong; him and Terry McKinney were our leaders.

* * *

Me da made a wooden frame covered in chicken wire and was fixing it over the outside of the front window. He was up on a chair.

'What's that for, Daddy?' I asked.

'Just in case there's any bother,' he said.

'What kind of bother?'

'Ach, you never know,' he said, hammering nails through the chicken-wire frame onto the wooden window frame.

I went inside to the front room. You could still see out. We'd be able to see the bother when it came. We didn't know what kind of bother he was talking about.

* * *

'Tony and Paul, yous are wanted quick,' said Karen to us as we played up near Moore Street. Moore Street was quieter now that us and the McKinneys had moved to Hamilton Street.

'Yous are wanted too. Your mammy's out calling yous in,' she said to Dooter and Jacqueline McKinney.

We all ran home. There was a smell of boiling cabbage in the house. There were a few bags full of clothes in the hall.

'The B-men are coming. They're going to invade,' said me ma, bustling about the sitting room.

'Is the B-men the police?' asked Paul.

Fear was in the air.

'Aye, the B-men. We have to go to your granny's,' she said.

'In Creggan?' I asked.

'Aye. Shut up the lot of yous till I get ready,' she snapped. 'Karen, make sure the lids are down right on them pots. Bring them out to the hall. I had to send for a taxi.'

This was the first of several flits from the Brandywell to me granny Sally's in Creggan.

Getting a taxi was exciting. It was a shiny, black, square-looking taxi. The driver wore a white shirt and dark tie. It was hot. We all got in the back seat. Me ma got in the front. She had Colleen in her arms. I was holding a frying pan with bacon in it. It sat on a newspaper on my lap. I could feel the heat coming through to my bare legs. There were pots on the floor of the car – we were having cabbage, bacon and mashed spuds for dinner – and bags of clothes. We passed McKinneys' house and their door was closed. Me da wasn't with us.

Me granny Sally's house had a long back garden with a single rose bush in it and hedges to divide it from the Edgars next door and from the gardens in Dunree Gardens below. My uncle Joe had asthma. He was only two years older than me so he wasn't really my uncle. He puffed on his inhalers when he was out of breath. 'Oh, me asthma. Oh, my ma,' he chanted when he wasn't really suffering from it, or when he was taking his inhalers. He went to bed when he suffered badly from it. Me granny said he 'had asthma all over his hands and arms' and it had to get wrapped in bandages and cream. My aunt Lorraine was younger than me so she wasn't really my aunt either; she was younger than our Paul.

We were show-jumpers out in the back garden. We set up jumps with brushes, mops and lengths of wood placed between buckets as fences. The hedges were jumps as well. Or we were boxers. We boxed with tea towels wrapped around our hands for mitts. I boxed our Paul until he cried out. Joe boxed me until I cried. Patrick boxed as well but he was too rough.

'There's the Yanks bombing in Vietnam,' said Granny Sally from her chair in front of the TV as pictures of jet fighters and huge explosions on wooded hillsides appeared on the screen. She drifted off to sleep and when she awoke again *Top of the Pops* was on the TV. 'Is that the Rolling Spuds?' she asked, pushing her brown-rimmed glasses up to her eyes. Everyone started to laugh. 'It's the Rolling Stones, Ma!' said Lorraine, and me granny's false teeth shot out of her mouth onto her chest as she let a loud laugh out of her as well.

We boxed on – Cassius Clay against Sonny Liston. Joe was the ref, shouting 'Box!' at the start and 'Break!' in the middle, or when we were in a tangle of tea towels.

* * *

Aunt Siobhán was in the kitchen with me granny and granda. She was older than Joe by a few years. They were arguing. I was sitting on a chair beside the cooker eating a piece and jam – mixed fruit jam. Siobhán was going to go down the town to the riots. She called them riots, but Sally and Connor called them 'royets'. She was wearing a multi-coloured overcoat and had a scarf wrapped loosely around her neck.

'You're not goin' down there and that's it!' said Granda Connor.

'Aye, I am! They said everybody's needed. Every woman and every man!' She was being defiant, standing up for herself. 'Anne Stewart's goin' down and so am I,' she said. She was raising her voice, but not shouting.

'You're goin' to git arrested. You'll be too slow to run from the B-men,' Granny Sally said. Siobhán was a heavy girl. 'Please Siobhán, don't go down.'

'They're firing CS gas by the square yard,' said Connor. He was half shouting, half pleading. Siobhán was winning. 'It'll choke the life out of ye!'

'I don't care what yous say,' said Siobhán, moving towards the kitchen door. 'I'm goin' down and that's it.'

And away she went.

Granny and Granda sat on at the table after she left. They made no attempt to follow her. They sat in silence. Me granny took a fag from the Embassy Red twenty-pack sitting on the table and lit it, sucking the smoke in deeply and letting it out with a long, deep sigh. The smoke came out down her nose and through her mouth. The early afternoon sun caught the white plume in its rays.

'That's nothin' but a cheeky bitch, that wan,' said Granda to no one in particular, the resignation obvious in his voice.

Granny Sally smoked her fag. There was no more to be said.

Granny Sally had huge silver pots. They were a lot bigger than our pots in Hamilton Street and they were used for chicken soup, stew, mushy peas and spuds (not all in the same pot!). Her teapot was far bigger too. In silence, befitting the occasion, I got up from my chair and went out to the street. My jam piece was done.

I was sent to the shops in Central Drive for messages. At Barr's I had to get plain flour, sliced hard cheese, buttermilk and a fine-toothed comb. Dozey Ford came along with me. The Fords lived a few doors up the street from me granny. Dozey was the same age as me. He was great craic. He always mimicked his mother talking. She had white hair and looked like his granny. The Fords' house was the same as me granny's with the wee round porthole window on the wall beside the front door. They had a dog called Rusty. Rusty Ford. Rusty came to the shops too.

A crowd had gathered on Bishop's Field, just opposite the shops. We crossed the road to the field to get a better look. There was a man with long hair and a beard standing up on something and speaking to the crowd. He was very nervous.

'The men down there, down the Bog, are under wild pressure,' he called out hoarsely. 'The police are forcing them back. If they break into the Bog they'll come for Creggan as well. Ye's need to get yourselves out of the bookies and out of your houses. Now, if I get down from here and run down that hill there towards the Bog, will you all follow me?'

'Aye!' some of the crowd shouted back to him.

'The men are desperate down there for help! Will yous follow me now or not?' he called out again.

'Aye,' shouted more of the crowd.

'Well, let's go then!' he called out and made to run down the field towards the New Road. Everyone ran after him. So did me and Dozey and Rusty, until we got near the bottom. I had the bag of messages in my arms.

'Dozey, me granny'll kill me if I don't bring her messages back,' I said.

'So she will, Tony,' he replied and we stopped.

'Hi you, young Ford,' some man shouted to Dozey. 'Git back up that hill or I'll put me boot up your arse!'

We ran back up the hill towards Barr's shop. We looked

back and the crowd was disappearing from view down the New Road. There were still a lot of people hanging around the field and the shops.

* * *

Granny Sally spread the newspaper on the floor near the hearth and we took turns. The light was on and so were her thick, Coke-bottle reading glasses. Joe was first to bend his head over the paper. She knelt down behind him and worked the fine-toothed comb through his thick brown hair. She said he had hair like a Brillo pad. The nits made a light pattering noise, like drizzle, as they crash-landed from his head onto the newspaper. You could see the wee brown spiders easier if they landed on a dark piece like an advertisement. He was then sat under the light as me granny went through his hair looking for nits and cracking them between the nails of her two thumbs. Me ma came in from the kitchen and joined the inspection line.

Patrick was next. He had black hair like me da. Me ma did the fine-tooth combing and me granny did the searching with her glasses on. Then it was my turn. I had fair hair. The fine-toothed comb hurt when it was dragged across your scalp. The nits fell from my head onto the paper. You heard them first and then saw them. The new ones were a lighter colour than Joe's and Patrick's. They walked very slowly. After me ma finished I got down between me granny's knees as she sat in her chair and I felt her fingers search through my hair for the smaller nits and eggs. She cracked their spines right beside your ear and rubbed the dead bodies on her trouser leg.

After about ten minutes, Granny Sally said, 'That's you finished now, Tony,' and Paul took his place between her knees.

Me ma gathered up the newspaper in her hands, taking care to fold in the edges. She scrunched it up, placed it in the empty hearth and put a match to it. It went up in a ball of flames.

* * *

It was night time. We were put to bed. The heat was fierce so we only had a single sheet covering us. Nobody could sleep with the heat. Sweat ran down our legs. All the teenagers – my uncles Michael and Gerard and aunt Siobhán were out, down the Bog at the 'royets'. There was a noise downstairs of someone coming into the house. Someone was singing. Connor was singing 'Sally' to Sally. We ventured out of the room in our underpants to listen at the top of the stairs. Karen and Lorraine were already there in their drawers and vests.

'He's been over in the Telstar all night,' whispered Lorraine, giggling. 'He must be bluttered.'

As well as the strains of song, the smell of fish and chips wafted up from below.

'C'mon yous all down,' called Sally from the hall.

After putting on vests and trousers we all clattered down-stairs to the sitting room. A feast of red (smoked) and white (unsmoked) battered fish and chips awaited us on the coffee table. Sally divided it into roughly equal portions on news-paper. More salt, more vinegar and glasses of Coke.

'No Coke for that boy,' said Karen nodding at Paul. 'We'll all be floating down the stairs in the morning.'

He was about to cry.

'Ach, give wee Paul a wee glass,' Connor slurred. 'He'll not pee the bed, won't you not, Paul.'

Paul looked happy again.

We all sat and ate and watched the TV, though Connor was more entertaining. He had on a grey pinstriped suit with a tie that had been loosened at the neck. As he sat deep in his chair you could hear the coins trickle from his pockets onto the seat. He paid no attention to it.

'Sing us a song, Da,' said Lorraine through a mouthful of chips.

'Ach, I could sing with the best of them in my day,' he replied. His nose and cheeks were red. He was a big strap-ping man with a full head of jet-black hair combed back like Humphrey Bogart. 'I sang wi' Josef Locke. He wasn't as good a chanter as me,' he said, smiling.

'Is that right?' I asked me granny. I didn't know who Josef Locke was.

'He did,' she replied. 'Your granda sang wi' Josef Locke.

That was years ago – in the thirties, before the war. Joe Mc-Laughlin we called him before he changed his name.'

'What did you do in the war, Granda?' I asked.

Sally laughed and answered for him. 'Oh, your granda was part of the suitcase brigade.' Both of them giggled. Sally was laughing at him but he looked away.

'I fought a red-headed nigger in Sarajevo,' he said, smiling broadly.

'What's that, Granda?' I asked.

'What's what?' he said.

'What's a red-headed nigger in Sarajevo?'

'A black man wi' red hair. I boxed the head off him in Sarajevo during the war,' he replied with a light laugh.

'Did ye really?' I asked, intrigued.

He just kept smiling and so did Sally.

The battered and smoked red fish was greasy and delicious. So were the chips. The extra salt and vinegar worked a treat. Connor had finished eating. Sally was watching him through half-closed eyes. There'd be no more songs from him tonight. Sally gathered the greasy papers in a ball in her hands and placed them in the hearth where the greasy paper burned fierce and bright for a minute.

'C'mon you, up to your bed now,' said Sally moving across the room in Connor's direction. He was starting to nod off and his head shot to attention at the sound of her voice. 'Joseph and Karen, give me a hand wi' him. He's fit for nothing.'

'C'mon you, up ye get!' she commanded.

'Aye, all right. God bliss us and save us – can a man not enjoy his drink?' he said with a slur, sitting forward in his chair to get up. As he rose Sally grabbed one arm and Joseph grabbed the other. They steadied him and moved towards the door. Karen followed behind them.

'Hold on a minute, hold on a minute would ye!' he said in a raised voice. 'Wait till I give the wains something.' He reached into his back trouser pocket. 'C'mon over here, wains,' he beckoned us with his hand.

We approached one by one and he placed a large green pound note into each of our hands. Sally was red-faced but said nothing. On they went – to the toilet first, where he farted, rifted and pished loudly with the door half open, humming to himself, and then upstairs, slowly clumping until you heard the creak of the bedsprings above.

Sally came back downstairs with Joe and Karen.

'Right,' she said. 'Hand me all the pound notes back. He must've made a rise at the bookies the day. He tells me nothing and gives me less.'

The party was over. We handed back our big green notes, which she bunched together in her hand.

'Yous can take that,' she said, nodding to where Connor had been sitting.

A scramble to the seat revealed a tidy sum of around ten bob in assorted coins under the cushion. It hadn't had time to slide down below the springs and fabric.

'And here,' she said, wagging her finger, 'not a word to your granda in the morning or yous'll dear bye it.'

We all nodded our assent and went back to our hot beds. There wasn't a word in the morning. Anyway, there was no sign of Granda Connor as the morning turned to midday.

* * *

The Cropie at the end of Central Drive was a massive green roundabout with grass on it. Cars drove around it and we played on it. There was a flat patch in the middle where we could play football. We had to be careful that the ball didn't run off the Cropie down Westway, as it wouldn't stop. The Cropie swarmed with wains, mostly boys playing football; girls played in the long grass around the pitch.

Danny Friel's nickname was Celtic. Danny Celtic. He was older than me but the same size, and he had dark red hair. He was a brilliant footballer. He could dribble the ball around everyone on the pitch. It was great to be on his team. Martin Stewart had dark red hair as well, but he was bigger than us. He supported Celtic too, but he was just called Martin, not Martin Celtic. Joe, my uncle, supported Manchester City. Joe was the same age as Martin Stewart but wasn't as good at football; his asthma held him back. Dozey Ford supported Spurs. I supported Manchester United then because of Georgie Best. I had a red Man United jersey with a white collar band and cuffs. Other boys from Dunree Gardens – the O'Hagans and the Morans – came over to the Cropie for football as well.

The Cropie was big enough to hide in and snipe from. It was Japanese (Japs) against Americans; the Cropie was the jungle. Teams were determined by height. One team would stay put to hold the fort and the other would fan out across the Cropie's expanse. Martin Stewart was the tallest so his team were the Americans fanning out. He was the captain. Danny Friel was small so he was the Jap captain. I was a Jap as well, along with Whitey O'Hagan and his wee brother. We were all short like Japs. Uncle Joe was the only one with a real cowboy gun and he was an American. He got the best of everything because of his asthma. The rest of us had long sticks. Our grenades were invisible. You just unhooked one from your t-shirt, pulled the pin out with your teeth, threw it at the enemy and made your own explosion noise.

Us four Japs were facing out of our smoothed-down grass fort in different directions, holding our sticks to our shoulders and pointing. The long grass rustled as the Americans approached. A shot rang out. It was Joe's cowboy gun.

'You're fucking dead, Whitey, ya wee Jap bastard,' called Joe from behind the long grass.

'Ye fuckin' missed me,' Whitey replied. 'It bounced off me helmet.'

'You don't have a helmet, ye've only a beret,' shouted Joe

and fired two more live caps at him. 'You're fuckin' dead now, ya Jap bastard!' He was a wild curser, as bad as our Patrick.

Whitey said 'Aahhhh', held his belly and fell over and died.

We started firing back with our machine guns into the grass. 'Rat-tat-tat-tat-tat-tat-tat-tat-tat' we all went.

'Yous haven't got machine guns, only rifles,' shouted Martin Stewart from the long grass.

'Aye we do. We have Jap riddley guns,' shouted Danny Friel defiantly and continued firing.

The sound of gunfire could be heard from behind the long grass. They were getting closer. Dozey Ford knelt upright and fired at Danny Friel. I fired back at him and he got down again.

'Dozey, you're got. I got ye,' I called out.

'Naw I'm not got. Ye missed,' he replied.

'Okay, men,' Martin called out in a John Wayne drawl, 'we're gonna wipe this Jap fort out.'

We Japs hadn't a chance against the advancing and better-equipped American forces. More rustling in the grass meant they were getting closer. It was hopeless being a Jap. Suddenly they were firing on all sides. While we fired back – 'bang bang bang … bang bang bang' – the Americans simply refused to die. When the big Yanks got up to overrun the fort we had no choice but to go 'Aahh!' and fall over and die. The Americans prodded us with their guns as we lay still on the ground to make sure we were dead.

Joe poked me with his muzzle in the back.

It hurt and my dead body kicked at him and missed. 'That's too hard,' I shouted, sitting up in the grass. 'Pack it in!'

The other dead Japs were still dead.

'You're dead, ya wee Jap fucker,' he said, poking me again in the chest.

'Japs and Americans is a load of shite. And stop pokin' me with that cowboy gun. It's not even an army gun.'

'The Americans can use any gun they want,' he replied.

'Well, I'm not playin' again. It's not fair.'

'You won't be playin' again. You can't take your fuckin' oil.'

'I'm tellin' me granny that you're over here cursing.'

'Tell her whatever the fuck ye like,' he said and walked away with his Yankee friends, his cowboy gun over his shoulder.

Everyone had gone in. I was on my own lying flat in the long grass looking at the pure blue sky. When you lie down in the long grass no one can see you from the street. I sat up facing down Westway. I could see beyond the city towards Magilligan Strand on one side of the water and Greencastle on the other, places I'd never been to. People say you can see the coast of Scotland from here on a clear day. This was a clear day and Scotland was nowhere to be seen.

A black man with black hair and wearing black clothes was walking up Westway towards the footpath round the Cropie. As he got closer he looked in my direction sitting up in the long grass.

'Hi boy, what are ye doin' over there on your own?' the black man asked. His teeth were very white.

'Daddy!' I called back.

It was me da, back from the riots down the Bog. He'd been away for three or four nights. I ran across the road to meet him and he gave me a tight hug.

'Why are you black, Da?' I asked. He looked like he was covered in soot and dark oil.

'Sure I'll tell yous all later. Let's go home.'

He took my small white hand in his huge black hand and we walked up to Granny Sally's house. When we got to the steep steps at the front everyone came out to meet us. The riots were over. The B-men were beat. The British Army had moved in.

Me ma made him a fry. He had a bath and went to bed. So did me ma.

* * *

'We stayed in Finner Camp. It belongs to the Irish Army,' Dooter told me and Paul. 'So did the O'Donnells.'

I felt robbed. An Irish Army camp! We were back in Hamilton Street. There was a lot of people milling around. The fear had gone. Me da was taking the chicken wire down from the front window.

'The soldiers let us hold their guns. Our Terry fired one,' Dooter added.

It got worse. All we did was play football in the Cropie and go to the shops and get our hair fine-tooth-combed for nits.

'They said for us to come back again. Me ma said we're goin' back next year,' Dooter went on.

'There's a fleadh the night up the lane,' said Gutsy.

'What's a fleadh?' I asked him. Gutsy was always in the know.

'I dunno, a party or somethin',' he replied. 'The Da Willies are playing.'

'The Da Willies? What's The Da Willies?' I asked. It sounded funny, like dickies.

'I think they're a band,' he replied. 'We're allowed up late for it anyway.'

'The Da Willies! The Da Willies! The Da Willies! The Da Willies!' we shouted for the rest of the day. It became the answer for everything:

'What are you gettin' for your tea?'

'A Da Willie!'

'What's your ma's name?

'Da Willie!'

'Will we play marlies later?'

'Da Willies!'

The fleadh turned out to be a concert staged on the back of a coal lorry positioned between Moore Street and Hamilton Street. Gutsy was right – The Da Willies *were* a band. They all had long hair and some had beards. One played a banjo. Others played on the accordion and tin whistles. They sang about the Cork and Kerry mountains and meeting Captain Farrell. They also sang 'The Black Velvet Band'. The crowd stood looking up at the band. Some were dancing with their hands up. Gutsy's da was drunk. He wore tinted glasses and his hair was combed back from his sharp face. He looked like Count Dracula. Gutsy's ma was there too but kept her distance, watching him. We were allowed out late. It was long past dark when we were called in for the night. The fear had gone.

* * *

Someone brought a magazine into the house to show me ma and da. There was a picture of me da on the front with flames and smoke in the background. A lorry was on fire. He was wearing a helmet and carrying a petrol bomb. His face was dark but it was definitely him. He was smiling and his lip was curled up like Elvis. He was looking away, but he seemed to know he was being photographed.

'Our street's in Free Derry,' said Gutsy.

'What's Free Derry?' I asked him.

'It's where the police aren't allowed into any more,' he replied. 'The army can only come to the foot of the street but they have to ask to get in.'

'Who do they ask?' I said.

'I dunno,' he shrugged.

Men wearing white armbands stood guard at the foot of the street. They were unsure of themselves and smoked. We played football around the gable. Someone had painted over the Moore Street sign with black paint and written 'Hooker Street' beneath it with the same paint. No one knew why or knew what Hooker Street was supposed to mean.

The army arrived in large, green, canvas-covered lorries. They sat for a while on Foyle Road, at the bottom of our street. A tall soldier in a peaked cap was the first to get out. He spoke to one of the men wearing armbands. We couldn't hear what they were saying but they were standing face to face. A few minutes later the tall officer approached one of the green lorries, pulled a couple of levers and opened the metal gates at the back. Soldiers jumped out. They carried rifles and one had a machine gun with bullets sticking out its side. Other green canvas-covered lorries were parked at the end of Moore Street and Anne Street. Soldiers were jumping out of all of them. Most wore helmets, strapped under the chin, like you saw in war films; some had dark berets on their heads.

The soldiers on Hamilton Street began taking sandbags out of the back of the lorry, two men to each sandbag, and placed them on the ground on the corner. They stacked them on top of each other like building bricks. A woman from the street arrived with a tray of china cups and a plate of sliced apple cake. A young girl behind her carried a china teapot.

'Ye's want a wee drop o' tea, boys?' she asked.

The soldiers, most of them looking like teenagers and one of them black, stood still, unsure what to do, and looked towards the officer in the peaked cap.

'Take the tea, chaps,' he said, approaching the woman and giving her a broad grin.

The woman smiled back and offered him the tray. He took it from her hands and held it while the woman, smiling, took the china teapot from the girl and poured the tea.

'Come on, chaps, don't be shy!' he called out, and the soldiers approached, smiling, and took a cup of tea; some took a triangle of apple cake.

Everyone smiled.

There was no apple cake for us. More women arrived with more tea, buns and biscuits. By this time there was a crowd at the end of the street. The soldiers had stood their rifles in a neat row up against the gable wall, the muzzles pointing up.

'They're SLRs,' said Terry McKinney.

Gutsy agreed. 'You can tell from the handle. There. Look.' He pointed his finger at the wooden handle sticking out from the metal piece in the middle.

'What's SLR stand for?' I asked.

Terry and Gutsy looked at each other and said they didn't know. A swarm of boys gathered close, eyeing the SLRs. They were a curious mix of polished wood and grey-blue metal. The wood looked out of place beside the metal pieces in the middle where the magazine was. A young soldier was left to guard the SLRs. He had no tea as he still had his rifle in his hands.

'Hi, what's SLR stand for?' Gutsy asked him.

'You wha'?'

'What's SLR stand for?' Gutsy repeated.

'Self-loading royfils,' the soldier replied.

'Self-loading royfils!' said Gutsy, mimicking his accent. Then he turned back to us: 'Oi! Self-loading royfils!'

The soldier smiled back at us in a nervous, uncomfortable sort of way, as if he'd be unsure what to do if we did something. He kept looking towards the soldiers taking their tea. Other women from the street had come out of their houses, some with plates of sandwiches and more pots of tea. They were all laughing – soldiers and all. And drinking tea.

'The soldiers have built a hut at the end of the street,' said Paul the next morning.

We were in the scullery, standing around the table – we had no chairs.

'They call them sangars,' said me da. 'Not huts.'

Me ma came in and poured herself a bowl of Special K and milk. The Special K box had a big red K on the front. We weren't allowed Special K – it was for me ma's diet.

She sat down. 'I must take them soldiers somethin' down the day. I'll make them ham and cheese sandwiches,' she said.

'You're not takin' anything down to them Limey Bs,' me

da said, looking her straight in the face. 'Them boys aren't here to protect us. They'll get nothin' from this house.'

'What are you on about – Limey Bs?' she asked. 'They *are* here to protect us. That's why they were brought in.'

'What's a Limey B, Da?' asked Paul.

'A Limey is an English soldier,' me da said. I could see he was annoyed with me ma. 'A Limey is a Limey. They never change. They're not here for our good.'

'Aye they are, Paddy,' me ma said. 'They're here to keep the B-men and the Paisleyites from doing their worst.' She wasn't for backing down. 'The poor soldiers only have army rations to eat. I'll get them some stuff in the shop later.'

'Listen to me now, Eileen. They'll get nothing from this house. Them Limeys will turn on us. You can't trust them. They're nothing but Limey Bs.'

'That's oul guff, Paddy. Wise up,' she said and put a spoonful of Special K in her mouth.

'Well, we'll see,' said me da.

Paul looked at me. Me ma had won.

The sangar was built at the end of our street on the corner with Foyle Road. It was built around the end house and it went around the corner. Its walls were made of sandbags. Some of the sandbags were damp and smelled of canvas. It had wooden posts for a doorway and a shiny, corrugated-metal roof. The soldiers could see up our street and both ways along Foyle Road. They also built sangars on the corners of both Moore Street and Anne Street. Gutsy said there were sangars further down Foyle Road as well.

'I went to the shop for one of them last night,' he said as we approached our sangar. 'The boy gave me two bob for going.'

'Why did he not go himself? Sure it's only over the street,' I said.

'They're not allowed. They cannae go up the street.'

'Hi mister, d'ye want us to go to the shop for ye?' I asked one of them.

There were four soldiers in the sangar, sitting on the ground reading newspapers. Their SLRs were lined up against the wall of the house.

'Yeah, moyt,' said one back and he reached into his pocket and brought out a green pound note. 'Get me a bottle of lemonade – cream soda – and a Flake,' he said, handing me the money.

We laughed at his accent. It was like *Blue Peter*, only different.

'Anybody else want anything in the shop?' asked Gutsy.

They looked up from the ground and one said, 'No, maybe later.'

Me, Gutsy and our Paul went to the shop. McLaughlin's shop was just up the street. We all went in. It was dark inside, as usual. There was an old woman behind the counter.

'Give us a bottle of cream soda and a Flake,' I said, placing the pound note on the counter and sliding it towards her.

'Is that for the soldiers?' she asked.

'Aye. One of them gave me two bob for going to the shop last night,' said Gutsy.

'Righty-o,' she said and reached behind her for the Flake. 'Go an' lift a bottle of cream soda from the crate there by the door.'

Several lemonade crates were lined along the wall near the door. I went and lifted the cream soda out of one and brought it back to the counter. Gutsy took a hold of the bottle as I reached for the change.

'This is my message, Gutsy,' I snapped. Gutsy was smaller than me. 'Here, give me that and you take the Flake. I have to bring him back his change.'

Gutsy handed the bottle back and out we went back towards the sangar. The soldier smiled as we approached. I handed him the cream soda and the change, and Gutsy gave him the Flake.

'Oi, Tony, give us a drink of lemonade,' said one of the soldiers sitting on the ground.

'Fack off and get yer fackin' own,' said Tony the soldier, laughing.

'Hi, ye call him Tony as well, so ye do,' said Gutsy pointing at me.

'Here you are then, Tony,' said Tony the soldier, handing me a shilling from the change. I smiled and took the coin from his hand, feeling a bit disappointed. Tony the soldier noticed the look in my eyes and said, 'Is that alroyt, moyt?'

'Gutsy got two bob last night for going to the shop,' I said.

'Who's Gutsy?' he asked.

'I'm Gutsy,' said Gutsy. 'I got the two bob.'

'Alroyt then,' said Tony the soldier, smiling, and handed me another shilling. 'Thank you, Tony.'

'Dead on, hi!' I said, feeling rich.

Tony the soldier was pouring the cream soda into metal cups on the ground when we left to head back to the shop.

The sangar and the soldiers became the centre of attention on Hamilton Street. We played football at the bottom of the street next to it, instead of up the street. Women, including me ma, brought them tea, buns and sandwiches in relays. The local men were civil to the soldiers but distant. Officers were ferried to and from the sangar in dark green, open-backed jeeps. When the officers were gone the soldiers allowed us to look down the sights of the SLRs, picking out people as targets as they walked along Foyle Road. Some of our targets laughed and waved back at the sangar, while others didn't seem to notice.

Chalk The Water came down the street on his donkey and cart.

'Chalk The Water!' we all called out to him. 'Chalk The Water!'

He waved his stick in the air and called something back. The soldiers looked on, smiling but not saying anything. Chalk The Water stopped at the junction beside the sangar. He didn't even look at the soldiers. He just looked out to see if anything was coming along Foyle Road, made a noise to the donkey and away they went.

'That's Chalk The Water. He's mad,' I explained, looking up at the soldiers. 'He drives out to the dump every day on his cart. D'ye want anything in the shop?'

'No, we're okay for the minute,' said one of them, smiling at Chalk The Water's donkey and cart.

It was trolley season. How seasons were determined I didn't know. The only season that was definite was conker season. That was in September, when conkers grew on the huge chestnut trees overhanging the high walls of the College on Bishop Street. Trolley season just happened, a bit like marlie season. The marbles just appeared in bags in the shops and then it was marlie season.

Trolley season required the hands and the know-how of Davy McKinney and Thomas Starrs, the big boys in the street. Davy was twice as tall as Thomas, but both were referred to as 'big boys'.

We had to cross Foyle Road to get planks of wood to build the trolleys – our Paul, Dooter McKinney, Terry McKinney and Davy McKinney. The McKinneys' dog, Dandy, came with us in case there were rats. People were dumping rubble there in mounds and all you had to do was pull the wood out from among the red bricks. We tucked our trouser legs into our socks in case a rat ran up and bit our dickies off. My uncle Joe once told me that when he had to go into hospital one time with his asthma, a man came in with a white towel around his neck. When the nurse removed the towel there was a huge rat hanging by its jaws from his throat.

Dandy sniffed around, her stubby sandy tail wagging in the air. The plank I wanted was buried deep and needed a few more boys to help pull it out. As we pulled at the dusty plank, sure enough a big mauser of a grey rat darted out from the rubble, ran up the plank and jumped over my shoulder.

'Holy shite!' I screamed, letting the plank drop and scurrying away in terror with my two hands up to my throat.

'Rats, Dandy! Rats!' called Davy McKinney to the dog.

Dandy chased it under another pile of rubble and was barking and scraping at the red bricks. Despite our deep fear of rats, we pulled at the rubble to help Dandy. The rat ran out from the back of the pile in panic and Dandy chased it along the open ground. The next pile of bricks and rubble was too far away – the rat was doomed. Dandy sprinted after it and caught it in her teeth, shaking it violently back and forth. The rat squealed in Dandy's mouth and then stopped. Dandy threw the rat up in the air and it landed with a thud on the dusty ground. It was still squirming a bit so it was still alive. Dandy scooped it up in her mouth again and shook it hard from side to side. The rat made no sound. Dandy threw it up in the air and this time it fell lifeless to the ground.

'Good girl, Dandy! Good girl,' said Terry McKinney as Dandy prodded the dead rat with her nose, inspecting it for signs of life.

'Wait till ye see this,' said Davy, lifting a boulder. He lifted it up over his head and brought it down on the dead rat. When he lifted the boulder the rat's skull was crushed and there was dark red blood on the ground underneath. He brought the boulder down on the dead rat again. When he lifted it there was no sign of further damage.

'Can we take turns?' I asked, and we all stood around the dead rat with boulders in our hands, bringing them down one by one on its lifeless body.

Eventually the rat's belly split to reveal a mass of pink and red, which looked strange against its dark grey coat.

'That's its guts,' said Terry, pointing to a tangle of squashed flesh after we'd finished pummelling it.

When we left with our planks, carried between two of us, Dandy jumped up on Davy and Terry's plank, her tail wagging, and we returned to Hamilton Street in victory.

The wheels for the trolleys were recovered from old prams, along with their axles. You really needed large wheels for the back and small ones at the front in order to go faster. The wooden planks became the chassis for the trolley.

For the front axle you required a brace and bit. The only

people who knew what the brace and bit were and how to use them were Davy and Thomas. Davy operated the brace and bit, and Thomas held the chassis plank steady for him to drill it. As many as ten boys were in the street with their planks and wheels. Everything was ready except for the fixing of the front axle to the chassis. For that, you needed a large nut, bolt and washers to attach them.

One time, when there was no brace and bit to be found, Davy and Thomas brought out white-hot pokers from the fire in Davy's house and roasted holes right through the planks. Back into the house they went for over an hour as the pokers cooled down, and out again with the white-hot pokers held high until all the planks were bored right through, with the heat and the smell of scorched wood filling the air around us.

The larger wheels were fixed to shorter lengths of wood and nailed to the chassis at the back. Nails were hard to find and we usually combed the bonfire site on the waste ground between Moore Street and Hamilton Street or scoured the back lanes to find them. We hammered them into the short planks in two straight parallel lines. Placing the axle between the lines, we then bent the nails over it, making sure the axle had enough space so the wheels were free to spin round.

Then you needed to attach a short length of rope to either side of the front axle in order to steer, and a square piece of wood for you to sit on. You also had to fix a short length of wood across the chassis to keep your feet off the ground.

After greasing all the axles, Davy and Thomas declared each trolley roadworthy.

Hamilton Street was flat and so was Moore Street. We had to go up Bishop Street, which had a steep slope, to race down it without being pushed. We couldn't go too far up or the Bishies would stone us. We raced to the bottom and just flew out onto Foyle Road as there was no way of stopping once you got going. You could use your feet but you'd destroy your shoes. It was okay if your shoes were old. After a few goes down Bishop Street we changed position on the trolleys. Instead of sitting back, we lay headfirst and flat on the plank with the steering ropes in our hands. That way you could push with your feet at the start and then jump on flat, like it was a bobsleigh. It was faster that way and you could hear the rumble of your pram wheels on the road, as your ears were right next to them as they spun round.

The army moved into the Mex, a disused factory on Foyle Road next to the Daisy Field. They dismantled the sangars. The trolleys became a taxi service for the soldiers' messages to the shops. We cruised outside the new barracks and waited for one of the soldiers to call us over to the iron railing gates, which were sometimes open and sometimes closed. On the flat, if you had no one to push you, you knelt upright at the back of the trolley and pushed with one foot. You could build up a good speed that way and be back at the Mex with the fags, chocolate, chewing gum, lemonade or crisps within five minutes – an express service. The money was good. It usually worked out at two bob a trip. We called the soldiers by their first names: Dave, Pete, John and George. That was just some of them.

The army drove up and down Foyle Road in a number of different vehicles. As well as the three-tonner canvas lorries and the open-back jeeps, they also drove Pigs, Ferrets and Sixers. Most were painted dark green, but some were sandy-coloured. Me da said they were painted the same colour as the desert sand for camouflage.

Pigs were square, squat-looking armoured cars with long snouts that squealed when driven at any speed. They had look-out hatches at the front, sides and back, and their huge black wheels were bigger than us. Ferrets were like small tanks with their turrets and machine guns sticking out. They had lookout hatches too, and sometimes a soldier sat up on the turret looking down on the road. Ferrets looked like large toys from a distance. They made a different squealing noise from the Pigs. Sixers had six wheels the same size as the wheels on the Pigs. They were almost the same as Pigs only with shorter snouts and a turret on top near the front. Sixers had hatches on the front, back and sides, and their engines squealed too, sort of like the Pigs.

If we were out playing in Hamilton Street and heard the noise of an approaching engine on Foyle Road, we stopped and tried to guess what type of vehicle would go past the gap at the bottom of the street on its way to or from the Mex.

'That's a Pig, I bet yis,' said Gutsy.

'Naw, it's not, it's a Sixer,' said Paddy Brown, who lived next door to Gutsy.

We all looked down the street towards the gap and a Pig drove by.

'I told you it was a Pig. You owe me money,' Gutsy said to Paddy Brown, chancing his arm.

'I didn't take your bet. I only said it was a Sixer,' he said.

Me da and our Patrick were coming down the street from Lecky Road.

'Get yous all into the house,' me da said pointing towards the door. 'Gutsy, g'won you home, son. Patrick, go and get Karen and tell her to get home.'

Patrick ran up the lane. Me and Paul went into the house. Karen and Patrick came in shortly after. The green front door was closed after them.

'What's wrong, Daddy?' asked Karen.

'Just stay in and keep the door closed. That Gutsy Mc-Gonagle was mouthing to Patrick. The fucker's as full as a po.'

Someone knocked loudly on the door. We ran to the front window to see who it was. It was Gutsy's da. You called him Gutsy too. He was on a crutch. He knocked again on the door, using the brass knocker this time.

'Cripple bastard!' said me da in the hall.

Gutsy's da knocked hard on the door once more. Me da went out to the hall and opened the door. We heard a thump and saw Gutsy's da landing on his back out in the middle of the road. The front door closed again. Gutsy's da didn't move on the road; he still had his crutch in his hand. After a minute or two, he started shouting for his wife and tried to get up on his feet. Gutsy's wife came out of her house to help him. Me da told us to get away from the window and into the back room. Me ma wasn't in. Me da was breathing heavily and stayed in the hall waiting to see if Gutsy's da would knock again. He didn't, but we were kept in for a good while just in case.

* * *

'Paddy Brown said that I have to sing something to you,' said our Paul to Karen.

'Sing what?' she asked.

He started singing in an English accent, 'Did you ever, did you ever, see your sister in the raw?'

Karen laughed. 'That Paddy Brown's a dirty wee brute. Don't you let me da hear you sing that to me.'

'Why, what's it about?' he asked her.

'Never mind. Just don't sing that again or you'll be in bother,' she said.

* * *

The Military Police, or MPs as we called them, patrolled our street, a man and a woman wearing peaked caps with a red band and white belts. They had armbands with the letters 'MP' written on them and they carried a pistol in a holster attached to the white belt. They walked up our street from Foyle Road, went towards the Lecky Road and then, about fifteen minutes later, they came back down the other side of the street. They didn't speak to us. Gutsy said they didn't like us going to the shops for the soldiers. They were brought in to put an end to it. He also said there was a new regiment in the Mex.

'Your da was fighting wi' a soldier the other day. He battered him,' said Gutsy.

'Who battered who?' I asked.

'Your da battered the soldier – outside the Silver Dog. The soldier was mouthing and pointing his gun at him. Your da said to him to put his gun down to see how much of a big man he was.'

'And what happened then?'

'He put the gun down and your da beat the shite out of him. The other soldiers lifted him up and took him down the street. His nose was busted. You wanny see the blood, hi!'

'And what happened then?'

'Nothin'. They all just went back into the bar.'

No one took tea and cakes any more to the soldiers at the Mex. It was probably too far away to carry them. Older boys threw stones at the Pigs, Sixers and Ferrets as they drove along Foyle Road. The stones made loud, tinny noises when they struck. Some of the vehicles were splattered with different colours of paint from paint-bombs made with milk bottles and beer bottles. The Foyle Road was covered in splashes of paint where the boys had missed their targets or were too far away to hit them.

But no one said anything to us about running to the shop for the soldiers so we just kept on going up to the gate with our trolleys and waiting to see if anyone needed anything. We didn't know their names any more and they didn't know ours. They still bought plenty of sweets, lemonade and chocolate in the shop, though.

Marlie season came. They appeared in the shop in wee net bags. We used the money we got from the soldiers to buy them. Only older people called them marbles; it was marlies or boodlies to us. There were two marlie games. One was like pitch-and-toss, where the boy who threw the marlie that landed closest to the kerb was the winner. We played on the road as there weren't many cars in our street. Winner took all on the pitch. The other marlie game began with a circle drawn in the dust or dry muck below the kerb. You had to try and knock a marlie out of the circle with your own marlie. Some flicked their marlie out with their thumb; others simply tossed it with their finger and thumb. Gutsy was a great flicker – an expert. He rolled the marlie on his tongue, dried it with his fingers and shot it out with a flick of his thumb into the circle. If it connected with an opposing marlie, it sent it flying out of the circle. If you pushed a marlie out of the circle it was yours, and you got a free go. If you hit a marlie and yours bounced out of the circle you lost it to whoever owned the first marlie.

We made a bigger circle of players around the small circle drawn in the dirt by the kerb and took turns, going clockwise.

As we played outside our house me da came out of the front door. He carried a wooden frame with a rusty brown metal sheet attached to it. He went back in and came out with a chair and a hammer. He put the chair beneath the front window and got up on it and proceeded to hammer nails through the wooden frame into the window frame.

'What's that for, Daddy?' I asked him as he worked.

'Just in case there's bother,' he answered, not looking around.

I went into the front room to see the effect of this and, when the door was closed, it was completely dark, like night time. His hammering was fierce loud in the room.

When I went back out, Chesty Crossan was standing outside his cottage across the street looking over.

'Can you do one for me, Patsy?' he called over. He was in his white vest and you could see his white, hairy shoulders.

'Aye, surely,' said me da. 'I have timber and metal sheet left over out in the yard. I'll bang it together and come over later to put it up.'

'That's dead on, Patsy. I'll sort you out with a few bob when I get me money,' said Chesty.

'Indeed you will not, Chesty. I'll be over later. Looks like more bother is on its way.'

'It does, Patsy. More bother surely,' said Chesty, looking down the street towards Foyle Road.

5

TRACERS

'Paul, are you wakened?' I whispered, nudging him.

I was seven and Paul was six. It was 1970.

'Aye.'

'There's a riot out in the street.'

'I know. I can hear it.'

Me ma had warned us not to go near the curtains if there was bother out in the street. We just lay on the beds and listened. Patrick and Karen were wakened too. You could hear the tin bin-lids clashing off the concrete footpaths around the Brandywell. This was the warning signal that the army was coming in.

'Limey bastards!' someone roared below our window.

There was the sound of running feet and glass smashing on the road. Dogs were barking in the yards of nearly every house – not ours; we didn't have a dog. Then there was a loud bang. From a gun? Within a short while my eyes started to itch. I rubbed them with my hands and they started to sting even worse. Patrick's and Karen's and Paul's eyes were burning too. My nose and throat were burning as well. We all started to cough. Paul began to cry.

Me ma came in. 'C'mon downstairs quick,' she said. She was holding wee Colleen on her hip. The baby was squealing and had a cloth over her face.

We all ran downstairs and into the sitting room. Me da was stuffing coats under the front door.

'What's that, Mammy? What's going on?' asked Karen, whose eyes were roaring red and streaming with tears.

'That's tear gas the army is firing. Here, put that over your face for a minute,' said me ma, handing her a white cloth from a basin in the kitchen sink. We all got one too. 'Not over your eyes – just your nose and mouth.'

We all stood under the light in the kitchen breathing, coughing and spluttering through the white cloths covering our mouths and noses. The cloths smelled of vinegar. The burning wasn't as bad now. The noise from the riot in the street wasn't as loud in the kitchen but you could still hear it.

Me da came in. His eyes were roaring red as well and he was coughing sorely into his hands. He went to the sink and ran the water into his cupped hands, which he then rubbed into his eyes.

'Limey bastards,' he said, still bent over the kitchen sink in his white vest. He stood up and lifted a cloth from the basin and held it over his nose and mouth and breathed deeply through it. 'I think they're moving up towards the Lecky,' he said to me ma. 'Imagine them Limey bastards shooting that stuff into the street. They're fuckin' worse than the B-men!'

There was no sound now except Colleen snivelling. Me da was listening at the front door to see what was going on out in the street.

'Right,' he said after a minute. 'C'mon and get your faces washed under the tap.'

We took turns splashing the water over our faces and around our eyes. Every one of us had purple-red eyes as if we all had the flu.

The next morning we were all sent to school. The street was littered with stones and broken glass, and there was a smell of burning in the air. As the four of us walked along Hamilton Street towards Foyle Road and Bishop Street, picking our way through the rubble and mess, our Paul lifted a coloured cardboard cylinder and sniffed it. Then we all took a sniff. It smelled of tear gas.

As we came out of Hamilton Street, there were six or seven assorted British Army vehicles on Foyle Road – Pigs, Sixers and Ferrets. The soldiers were standing in the road with helmets on and carrying rifles and shorter black guns with wooden butts.

'Limey bastards,' hissed our Patrick as we passed.

Some of the soldiers sneered back but didn't say anything. Some of them we knew from the Mex and they smiled at us, but we didn't smile back. As we got further up Bishop Street towards the Long Tower, Patrick turned around and called 'Limey bastards!' down towards the soldiers. A few of them laughed and gave us the fingers. Our Patrick was a wild curser.

When I got into the classroom, someone had given a black rubber bullet to the teacher, Mr McLaughlin. The boy had found it on his way to school. It stood up on Mr McLaughlin's desk pointing to the ceiling.

Joe Mooney said it was a rubber dickie. At break time we all gathered round it to touch it and bounce it on the wooden floor. It bounced all over the place and shot away at curious angles.

'The BA fire them at the rioters. There was boys hit wi' them in our street. Ye wanny see the bruises, hi,' said Joe. Joe lived in Creggan. The BA was the new name for the soldiers.

'They were firing CS gas in our street all night,' I said to impress. 'Everyone in our house was chokin' wi' it.'

'It was the same wi' us too,' said Waybo, whose real name was Barry Wade. Waybo lived in the Bog. 'One landed right at our front door and me ma went out and threw a bucket of water over it and kicked it away. We were all as sick as dogs.'

After the break, Mr McLaughlin was standing by the blackboard talking when he became distracted by something going on behind us in the yard. The whole class turned round to see a group of soldiers in the yard through the windows behind us.

'The BA's in the yard!' someone shouted.

Mr McLaughlin walked towards the window. 'Stay where

you are and don't leave your desks,' he said and hurried out of the classroom door. We could hear other teachers in the corridor talking.

We all gathered around the three tall, panelled windows to look out at the BA walking through the yard. There were about twelve of them.

Satch Kelly, who was the headmaster, and a few other teachers including Mr McLaughlin, approached the soldiers in the yard. The soldiers all carried SLRs and some had the shorter rubber bullet guns slung across their backs. Satch had his arms out, pleading to the soldier in charge. They were the same height – both of them were tall and lanky. The rest of the soldiers and teachers were small. We could hear them speaking, but couldn't make out what they were saying.

The tall soldier wore black leather gloves and was sneering back at Mr Kelly. Mr Kelly was pointing towards the school gate on Bishop Street as if showing him the way out. The tall soldier turned away from him and went over to another soldier who had a map in his hands. Both examined the map while Mr Kelly looked on in silence.

The tall soldier approached Mr Kelly again, pointed to the front door of the school and gestured with his gloved hand to get back into the school. He held his rifle with the other hand. Mr Kelly was red-faced with anger.

Mr Kelly's son, Owen, was in our class. He had carrotty red hair and his face was a mass of freckles.

'Your da's goin' to get himself shot,' someone said to him as we watched the argument in the yard.

Mr Kelly had taken his glasses off and put them in his top jacket pocket. The tall soldier had turned away again and a group of them stood near the rain shelter talking among themselves. Several of the teachers approached Mr Kelly, and then they all walked back towards the school. We all gave the soldiers the fingers through the window and they waved back at us, laughing.

A few minutes later Mr McLaughlin came back into the classroom. 'Right boys, come on away from the window and get back to your desks. We have work to do.'

We all sat down. The soldiers were still in the yard. Some of them had sat down in front of the shelter and were smoking and laughing, their SLRs lying on the ground beside them.

'What did Mr Kelly say to the big BA officer?' asked Joe Mooney.

'Never mind,' said Mr McLaughlin. 'That's not important. We have maths to do.'

* * *

A crowd, mostly young men, had gathered at the corner of Hamilton Street and were throwing stones at soldiers on Foyle Road outside the Mex. Teenage girls stood at the corner of Moore Street looking at the young men rioting. It was still daylight and me ma and da were still at work so we ventured down to the corner to see.

The soldiers were in the middle of the road, sheltering behind short, green, metal shields, which they held over themselves at an upward angle to protect their heads. They were banging the shields with long, wooden riot batons. The noise was fierce: wood on metal; brick on metal; bottles smashing on the road; cursing and shouting in angry tones.

'GET BACK TO ENGLAND YOUS TOMMY BASTARDS!'

'ENGLISH BASTARDS!'

The rioters shouted all sorts as they whizzed and lobbed their stones, and the stones rattled off the riot shields. A soldier jumped out and fired a rubber bullet into the crowd. At the sound, the rioters seemed to bend backwards as one, with their heads down and hands covering their heads, like flowers blown by a sudden wind. The 'rubber' went through the crowd and bounced off the wall of the second house on Hamilton Street, then bounced back across the street towards us. Me, Johnny Barbour, Gutsy and our Paul made a scramble for it even before it had stopped bouncing. Paul was first to snatch it in his hands, and he ran up the street with it held high like a football trophy. We ran after him, exalted, until we reached the house.

Paul held the rubber into his side, cradling it.

'Let us see it, hi!' said Johnny.

'Okay, but it's mine, okay? I grabbed it first,' said Paul, handing it over.

Tony's grandparents, Sally and Connor Quigley.

Tony's grandmother Sally with her first four children: Anna, Patsy (on her knee), Eugene and his mother, Eileen. Taken in 1947.

Eileen and Patsy Doherty in the yard of 6 Moore Street.

Patsy, with Colleen, Paul, Tony, Patrick and Karen out the Line
in 1969.

The Doherty family and friends at Aunt Margaret's wedding in St Mary's Chapel, April 1968. Tony's grandfather and grandmother, Paddy and Cassie Doherty, are at the front on the far left.

Eileen with Karen, Paul, Tony and Patrick up the bankin'
in 1968.

Some of the Dohertys and McKinneys in Moore Street in 1967.

Karen and Patrick Doherty.

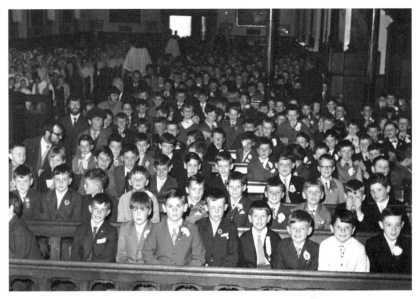

Long Tower Boys First Communion in the Long Tower Chapel in May 1971. Damien Harkin and Tony are both in the photo.

A Hamilton Street barricade. *Photo courtesy of Éamon Melaugh*

Patsy Doherty's mucker Eddie Millar at a
Moore Street barricade.

Tony (*left*) and
Paul Doherty.

Damien Harkin, Tony's classmate who was killed by a
British Army lorry.

British soldiers seek their bearings on Quarry Street in July 1971.
Photo courtesy of Jimmy Melaugh

Moore Street (*left*) and Hamilton Street in 1968.
Photo courtesy of Jimmy Melaugh

Johnny took it in his hands. It smelled strongly, like the smoke from fireworks or sparklers we got at Hallowe'en. Johnny threw it hard on the ground and it bounced away at a sharp angle for about fifteen yards. Paul ran after it and took it indoors to show me ma and da when they got in from work.

We went back down to the corner. The riot had got worse. There were more teenagers on the road throwing stones and, about seventy yards away, there was a pile of stones heaped on the road below the soldiers' shields. The lead rioters would sometimes run up close to the soldiers hunkering behind the riot shields and throw a stone before running back into the crowd. One rioter, wearing jeans, a denim jacket and black boots, was hit in the back with a rubber as he returned to the crowd. The bang was followed by a slap as the rubber hit him and forced him to the ground, rolling and writhing in pain. The soldiers, seeing their opportunity, ran out from behind the shields with their batons in their hands, screaming at the top of their voices. We, the spectators section at the back of the riot, all ran in a panic up Hamilton Street, but those at the front, the main rioters, didn't. Instead they kept throwing their stones at the oncoming soldiers, while two others lifted the wounded rioter, one arm each around their shoulders, and dragged him into Hamilton Street, his black boots trailing on the ground, and sat him up against the wall of a house.

The sound of rubber bullets firing continued around the corner on Foyle Road as those who had run away drifted back down Hamilton Street again towards the battle. A woman brought the injured teenager a glass of water, which he drank, white-faced and in obvious pain. A Pig had squealed into position across Foyle Road at the junction with Hamilton Street. Rubbers were being fired from its side hatches into the street. The woman and another man helped the teenager to his feet, led him into a house and closed the door behind them. The rubber bullets were flying up our street, and people jammed themselves into doorways and behind lamp posts to avoid them. A group of rioters brought several large rusted sheets of corrugated tin from the sheds behind our house and began manoeuvring towards the junction. They were beckoning others to follow when the soldiers inside the Pig and behind it fired a loud salvo of rubbers at the tin sheets. The sound of rubber on tin echoed up and down our street for what seemed like forever. Others missed and flew on up Hamilton Street, which drew a scramble for the rubbers as they bounced precariously off walls and onto the road.

A crowd of rioters had run up the lane towards Moore Street and a few minutes later you could hear the clang of stones on metal as they bombarded the Pig from a new angle. The soldiers firing from the front of the Pig were being pelted and ran around to the back for cover. The boys behind the tin sheets pelted them with stones and, in a panic, the soldiers tried to open the back doors of the Pig to get inside for cover. But the Pig took off up Foyle Road under the fusillade of stones, leaving the soldiers at the rear on their own. The rioters, seeing their opportunity, dropped the tin sheets and pursued them, firing stones and bottles at the fleeing soldiers. We decided it was safe enough for us to follow and, as we reached the street corner, we saw several dozen soldiers run to their new retreat position at the gates of the Mex barracks, where they regrouped.

Shouts and cheers of victory rang out from the rioters, and from the teenage girls watching from Moore Street.

'Your ma's back from work. Your Karen's calling you,' said Johnny Barbour in the midst of the happy cheering.

'C'mon you, boy, me ma's looking for all of us,' said Karen as she approached.

'I'm staying here. Tell her I'll be in later,' I said, turning away.

'Git you up to that house. I'm not going back without you or I'll be killed,' she said, grabbing me by the arm.

The sound of more rubber bullets firing sent us all back with our hands over our heads.

I had allowed myself to be taken from the riot by my big sister. The rest of them stayed on, spectating. It just wasn't fair. We lay in bed that night and could hear another riot outside and down towards the corner. The sounds were the same except for the occasional loud explosion, which rattled the windows and doors, and made the house shake.

'What the fuck is that?' our Patrick asked Karen in the dark.

They were in the bed across the room. There was real fear in his voice.

'Must be bombs of some sort,' she replied and we returned to our dark, scared silence.

* * *

One day, when me and our Paul were returning from school, we decided for some reason to go down the Folly instead of Bishop Street towards home. A small crowd of boys and girls had gathered on the corner where Hamilton Street met the top of Anne Street. As we got closer, we saw a group of five men sitting against the corner house wall with guns across their laps. They had masks over their faces with badly cut eye holes; some had a huge opening for one eye beside a tiny opening for the other, which made them look oddly distorted. They wore an assortment of green army coats and jeans. The guns weren't the same as the BA's guns; they were mostly wooden with only a few metal pieces.

Gutsy was there before us.

'Are yous the IRA, hi?' he asked one of them.

'Aye, we are,' was the reply.

'Are yous goney shoot the BA?' asked Gutsy.

'G'won away, Gutsy, and mind your own business,' said another.

'How do you know me, hi?' asked Gutsy.

'Never mind. Just stop asking questions,' he said.

'Is that a 303 you have there, hi?' Gutsy persisted.

'Aye it is, now g'won away,' he replied.

'Ach, hi, I'm only askin',' said Gutsy, offended, as he moved along the line.

'Your man there has a carbine,' said Gutsy, pointing to a smaller-looking wooden rifle with a tiny magazine, which looked like a toy.

'How do you know?' I asked, jealous that he knew all this stuff.

'I just know,' he said, brimming with confidence and in his element. 'That there wan is a Thompson,' he added, pointing to the man at the end holding a machine gun upwards with the butt on the pavement. His mask was made of grey wool and tied at the top with an elastic band.

Coming home from school by the same route a few days later we found that a concrete barricade had been built into the road at the top of our street. There were steel girders and poles sticking out of the concrete, as well as a farm gate. That night the Vigilantes kept everyone away from the concrete until it hardened. The Vigilantes were local men who guarded our street and other streets at night. They were not the IRA. The women in the street brought them tea and sandwiches and biscuits while they stood guard or patrolled up and down the street. At the other end of the street a huge pile of soil and rubble had been pushed onto the road. You could still walk on the pavement but not the road. An old lorry had been pulled across the road up in Moore Street. The BA drove slowly up and down Foyle Road in Ferrets, Pigs and Sixers.

* * *

It was a Saturday. Word got round that all the wains were to go to the Mex barracks in the afternoon for something the BA was going to do.

No one questioned it. None of us had ever been in the Mex before. We usually only went as far as the gate for the messages, and there had been fewer messages in recent times with the rioting. There was no rioting today. The road was clear. The gates of the Mex were open and we went through them.

Soldiers stood around in their shirtsleeves looking a bit unsure of themselves. We were guided into a large hall that had a snooker table and a table laden with cakes, buns, biscuits and lemonade. There were around twenty-five children there. A film was being projected onto a large screen against the wall – M*A*S*H. Soldiers were sitting on wooden fold-out chairs watching the film and looking round to watch us as well. We all sat or stood between the food table and where the soldiers were seated. On the screen there was a lot of blood as someone was being operated on. We had cake, and lemonade in large white plastic mugs. Paddy Brown and our Paul had green metal army helmets on their heads and were laughing and messing about with the soldiers. The sound of helicopters on the screen was very loud. A couple of wains were playing snooker with the soldiers. Another group of soldiers were standing at the doorway talking to the officer and looking out the door towards the gates.

Suddenly something hit the metal roof above us and bounced across it, followed by another. The soldiers, only slightly distracted, went back to watching *M*A*S*H*. Then there was another clump and clang on the roof. And another. The soldiers at the door grew nervous and called the officer over. The film was brought to a stop and the lights went on. More stones bounced across the roof. It was time to go. We filed out the door along the concrete path towards the locked gates. A large group of adults – parents and teenagers – were standing on the outside looking in. Some of the teenagers were throwing stones onto the roof, but they stopped firing when they saw us. The soldiers at the gates opened them as we approached.

Me ma and da were there. Me da, red-faced, went up to the officer walking with us and grabbed him with both hands by the shirt. The officer was about a foot taller than him. Other men grabbed me da from behind and pulled him away. We walked through the large group of parents and impatient rioters, and me ma and da followed us in silence up the street towards the house. As we walked along we looked at each other, wondering what the consequences were going to be. But when we got back to the house no one mentioned the Mex, not even me ma and da, and it was never spoken of again.

* * *

Me and our Paul went up to Moore Street to see Paddy Stewart. He always gave us money when he saw us. As we approached the green door of No. 6 we saw Paddy standing at the foot of the street with a group of older men. They were just standing, looking. It was a bright, warm, sunny day. Behind them, the river was a silvery blue.

'Hello, boys,' said Paddy with a smile as he saw us coming. He had his flat cap on, and he was wearing a dark purple cardigan with a shirt and tie.

'Hello, Paddy,' we said back, but he had stopped looking in our direction.

The group of older men seemed to be waiting for something to happen. There was something in the air.

Suddenly, a small open-backed truck with low sides came down Bishop Street and swung left onto Foyle Road. There were long-haired men wearing dark glasses and clutching machine guns squatting in the back of it. As it drove slowly up Foyle Road away from us, one of the men shot at a billboard advertising Special K that stood by the roadside.

You could see the smoke coming out of the barrel. The sharp sound of the machine gun – it was a Thompson – startled us, but no one dived to the ground. So that's what Paddy and his muckers were waiting for! The woman in the Special K advert was left with holes in her face and through her perfect white teeth.

'Cowboys!' said one old man.

'Boys-a-boys-a-boys!' said another.

'Cowboys? More like Comanches!' said another. 'He shot the Special K woman for Ireland!'

The old men laughed to themselves and the truck continued on down Foyle Road and out of sight. Boys the same age as us, Bishies, ran onto the road in front of the billboard and started picking things up. Me and Paul ran over to see as well. One boy had a number of small brass things in his hand.

'What's that, hi?' asked our Paul.

The boy held one up between his finger and thumb. 'They're bullet shells. That's what comes out of the gun after it's fired. Now fuck off back to Hamilton Street where yous belong!' he said and shoved our Paul in the chest.

'Hi boy. Leave the wee fella alone,' Paddy Stewart shouted over from the corner of the street.

'Aye, leave him alone,' I repeated, putting myself between him and Paul.

The Bishie looked at me, him with snotters caked to his upper lip and nostrils, and glanced over at Paddy Stewart and the group of men standing at the corner with their flat caps on.

'I'll get you later, you wee Hammy fucker!' he said and turned and headed back down Foyle Road with his gang, and a handful of brass bullet shells.

I wasn't wee at all. I was the same size as him.

* * *

The bankin' is flat at the top and a bit bumpy here and there. We decided we wanted to dig a hut for ourselves, and so a small army of Dohertys, Barbours and McKinneys headed to the bankin' with spades and shovels twice the length of us.

'We'll dig straight down,' said Terry McKinney, 'in a square.'

There was some corrugated tin lying at the back of Moore Street, so we gathered it up for our roof. The digging lasted the whole day. It had been raining, so the top sods were easy cut, but underneath the soil was hard and compacted. We sat the grassy sods to one side to use later. As there were too many of us, we took turns to dig. Someone brought biscuits and a milk bottle filled with water; there was a track of congealed milk on it. We ate the biscuits – Custard Creams and Ginger Nuts – and passed the bottle of water around. By the time it got to me – the third person, there were yellow and brown floaters in the water. No one mentioned it. We were dry so we drank. Down we dug in the hole, scooping out the brown soil with the shovels. The soil grew like a small hill beside the hole. Soon the workers were belly-height with the top of the hole.

'We have to be able to stand up inside it,' said Terry McKinney.

Terry knew everything, so the digging continued and the diggers sank further and further into the ancient bankin' until only their heads and shoulders could be seen at the top.

'A wee bit more and we're finished,' Terry said.

Soon the digging stopped and the hill of soil dumped at the side had become two hills. The rusty corrugated tin sheets were brought over to make the roof. A wooden post was loosely hammered into the rock-hard ground in the centre of the hole and the corrugated tin was placed on top in overlapping layers, with the wooden stake propping the whole lot up in the middle. The sods we'd cut earlier were placed back over the corrugated tin, camouflaging our hut from unwelcome visitors. A gap was left in the corner so we could get in and out, like a submarine.

As soon as the last layer of tin went on we all climbed in and sat around the sides of the hut, staring in wonder at the fruits of our labour. That's what the hut was made for – to sit in. A shower of sunlight came in through the nail-holes and gashes in the rusty tin sheeting. Our hands and faces, clothes and shoes were boggin' with dirt. This was luxury. This was what we'd made for ourselves. But it was nearly teatime, so we decided to leave the hut and go home, and to come back after our tea with candles and matches.

When we gathered there again after our tea, some of us had been washed clean by our mas; others looked like they'd tried to wash themselves and not made a good job of it. We all slid back into the hut. It wasn't as bright now, so we lit the candles and played cards in the dry dirt.

I was busting for a pee so I slid out of the hatch and walked a few yards away to do it. The light was fading and a dark grey pall was replacing the earlier brightness. After peeing I began to ease my way back into the hut, feet first. With only my head and shoulders at bankin' level, I looked up and saw two banshees emerging from the semi-darkness in the direction of St Columb's College and running towards us. By banshees I mean The Real Thing – white-sheeted bodies with black eyes.

'Jesus, Jesus!' I cried out as I heaved myself out of the hut again. 'There's two banshees running down the bankin'! Get out quick!'

There was a scramble of panicked movement as bodies emerged through the gap.

'Jesus! So it is!' said our Paul as he looked up to check. 'Get t'fuck out!' Our Paul never cursed.

Suddenly the sods and tin sheeting lifted from the other end of the hut and one of the Barbours scrambled out onto the grass. The banshees were about fifty yards away and closing fast, their billowing white bodies growing larger the closer they got. Everyone was out and running. There was panic and fear in our breath as we ran down the steep bankin' away from the banshees, who were very good runners.

Michael McKinney, brother of Dooter and Terry, slipped on the dirt track that led from the bankin' to the rear of Moore Street. The banshees were right behind him and I could hear his panicked squeals. As I ran I looked over my shoulder to see the banshees grabbing Michael as he tried to get up. They'd got him!

We ran like mad around the corner and down the lane towards the McKinneys' house. Hearing the commotion outside their front door, Maisie and Cecil McKinney came out to see what was going on.

'Our Michael's been kidnapped by banshees,' said Terry, out of puff and with real fear in his voice. 'They have him up the bankin'.'

Cecil looked at his wife and then took off around the corner towards the bankin'.

'Stay yous all here and tell me what happened,' said Maisie as we went to follow him. There was a hint of suspicion in her voice as if she thought we were up to something.

'What do think they're doing on him?' I asked Maisie, panting and ignoring her question. 'Do they just eat you?'

'I'm sure it'll be all right,' was all she said, looking towards the corner and waiting for Cecil to reappear.

It was now dark and the streetlights had come on. Around that corner, though, it was still dark, in the shadows of the last house in the terrace. Sure enough, a few minutes later – it seemed like a lifetime – Cecil and Michael came around the corner, Cecil with a hand on Michael's shoulder and Michael crying. We rushed towards them to see what the banshees had done on him. He had muck on his face, but he wasn't torn apart or anything.

'What did they do, Michael? What did the banshees do on you?' we asked.

Michael didn't say anything.

'G'won yous on home a' that. It doesn't matter what happened. He's all right now,' said his da, steering Michael in through the front door. 'C'mon yous in,' he said to Dooter and Terry.

The front door closed after them. We were left out in the dark, unknown world and made our way under a cloud of wonderment along Hamilton Street to our own houses. The kidnapping was never mentioned again.

A week or so later the BA came to the hut on the bankin'. Terry said there was a major and some soldiers. The major had climbed into the hut, asked one of the soldiers to give him his rifle and aimed it out towards the Line and the Mex. Then he declared the hut an IRA observation post and ordered his soldiers to fill the hut in. When we came up later, after Terry told us, the hut was gone. The tin sheets were strewn to one side and a small mound of newly dug soil like a new grave was all there was to see.

'Me da said we shouldn't dig it up again – for a while, anyway. The soldiers'll just come back and fill it in again,' said Terry, as we stared at the ground in disbelief.

'Limey bastards,' said our Paul as we turned, our heads low, to dander back down the hill towards the street.

One day I found myself walking alone from school along Hamilton Street. There were two men ahead of me, one on either side of the road. They were wearing green army coats and jeans and had long hair. They were talking to each other across the street. I couldn't hear what they were saying, but they were IRA men – you just knew. There was no one else on the street but us three. The one on the right, the one with dirty fair hair, reached into his side pocket and all of a sudden there was a small, dark gun in his hand, which he pointed across the street at his friend. They both laughed. The man with the gun saw me walking behind them and looked away, but he kept the gun in his hand pointing downwards towards the footpath. They walked past our house towards the corner with Foyle Road and then stopped. They looked back at me and I disappeared into the house to do my homework.

* * *

A lone soldier was on top of the high wall of the Mex, building a sangar with sandbags. The wall was about thirty feet high.

He was working close to the edge and it looked dangerous. It was a hot day and he was wearing his shirt open with no flak jacket. He had fair hair and was red-faced.

'Hi, d'ye want anything in the shop?' I shouted up at him from the road below.

I was on my own. I had no intention of coming back with his messages. That game was up but I thought I'd chance my arm.

'No thanks, moyt,' he shouted down at me while he continued stacking the sandbags.

'The shop's only round the corner. I could be back in five minutes for you,' I called up.

'No, thanks. I have all I need,' and he went on working.

'Where are you from, hi?' I shouted up to him.

'Leeds.'

'My brother Paul supports Leeds,' I replied. 'But they're shite,' I added, disappointed at not getting any money.

He laughed, looked down at me for a second and continued working. He wasn't interested. I dawdled about below the high wall in the heat for a few minutes and, deciding there was no point in making my offer to run to the shop again, I headed back up Foyle Road towards our street. As I passed the metal gates to the Mex a loud shot rang out. I hit the deck and kept my head down. It was aimed at the Mex; I could tell. It was fired at the soldier I'd been talking to; I just knew. They had been waiting for me to go away before they fired; I knew that as well. No more shots followed and none was returned. There was only silence and heat.

Then the silence was broken by a commotion on the roof of the Mex. I couldn't tell what they were saying but it sounded serious. I took my chance, got up on my knees and made a bolt for the corner of our street and safety. A few minutes later, a Sixer with a red cross on the side drove at speed from the Mex towards Craigavon Bridge.

* * *

Fishing for fluke (a flat fish like a flounder) is something we did when we had nothing else to do, usually on a Saturday or a Sunday.

Me, Kevin Morrison, Johnny Barbour and our Paul were out the Line, sitting on a low wall beside the river on a warm and overcast day. Our fishing equipment was a piece of stick with thick orange gut wrapped around it (the reel), a few hooks, a sinker and a float. We had a baked bean tin full of worms. The worms writhed in pain at being gored by the hook, but they were only worms. You then held the reel in your left hand and swung the line with the float, sinker, hook and worm on it around your head like a lasso and cast it into the brown water. The fluke were everywhere so you didn't need to cast that far.

We all cast out. It was a race to see who could catch the most. The fluke bit very quickly and you just wrapped the gut back around the wooden reel to bring them in, flipping and flopping in and out of the water as they realised they'd been caught. When you got your fluke in, you grabbed it and hit its head on the low wall until it was either dead or knocked out; it'll die soon if it's just knocked out. We laid out our dead in rows behind us as we sat on the low wall. The fluke we caught varied in size, from about the size of a twenty-pack of fags to a dinner plate. Sometimes the fluke came round after being knocked out and tried to flip off the wall back into their watery home. We laid the dead fish out, from the biggest to the smallest, along the wall and then counted them before we went home. We then threw them back in again before we packed up because we couldn't eat them.

After we'd thrown the fluke back in, we walked along the edge of the river towards home, then cut across the waste land between the river and Foyle Road. Suddenly I spotted a live bullet lying on the dry ground. As I picked it up I noticed that the bullet head was painted black at the tip.

'Hi boys, look at this!' I said holding the brass bullet up to show the other three. 'I found a live bullet, hi!' They gathered round to see it. It was heavy for being such a small thing.

'That's a rifle bullet, so it is,' said Kevin.

'What's the black paint for at the top?' I asked, pointing.

No one knew. We all rubbed it through our hands.

'What'll we do with it? We can't take it home,' I said.

We all agreed – we couldn't take it home.

'We could fire it over to the Waterside. There's an army barracks over there,' said Johnny, pointing across the river.

I couldn't see any army barracks, just trees.

'How do you fire it without a gun?' asked our Paul. 'We've no gun.'

'Put it on a hard stone and smash it with another hard stone,' said Kevin. 'There's a stone there.'

He went over and placed the bullet on the stone, with its black head pointing towards the Waterside.

'Who's goin' to do it?' I asked, feeling a bit scared. What if it goes off in the wrong direction, I thought, worried only about my own well-being.

'I'll do it,' said Johnny. 'Sure we can take turns until it goes off.'

He lifted a medium-sized boulder from a heap of rubble. We all stood behind him as he dropped the stone from shoulder height onto the live bullet. The bullet rolled off the flat stone onto the dry dirt. He missed. He must've meant to miss. You couldn't miss from that distance.

I then placed the bullet back onto the flat of the stone, pointing it again towards the Waterside. I lifted the boulder with my two hands. The fear had gone but I was still really scared inside. I raised the boulder over my head and brought it down heavily onto the bullet. It didn't go off. The boulder was too soft; it only made a chalky dent on the bullet's rounded metal.

'Don't do it any more,' said our Paul. We all agreed.

'What'll we do wi' the bullet?' I asked, picking it up and rubbing the dust from it.

'I'll take it into school and give it to the teacher,' said Johnny, holding his hand out to me. 'Everyone brings in stuff for the teacher.'

'What kind of stuff?' I asked, placing the black-headed bullet in his hand.

'You know, bullets and all,' he said.

'What else?' I asked.

'Somebody brought him in a live gas CS canister once.'

'Who?'

'Somebody from the Bog. I cannae remember who,' said Johnny.

As we were talking about how to get rid of the bullet we walked back across the dumping ground between the river and Foyle Road. When we reached the road a long, dark blue car was parked in the middle of the road just outside the Mex. There was no one near it. We didn't say anything, just kept walking across the road to the entrance at Hamilton Street, which had high mounds of rubble and clay on either side of the road, enough to slow cars down as they entered or left the street.

We neared our house and our Karen was at the front door crying, her hand over her mouth. She went inside when she saw us coming. Me ma was in but me da was out, and me ma was trying to comfort Karen, who was saying something about a man and a woman being shot in a car outside the Mex, that there was blood everywhere. Me and our Paul eyed each other, went quietly out the door, back out to the street and ran round the corner towards the Mex. The long, dark blue car was still in the middle of the road and there was still no one near it. A few wains had gathered at the roadside to gawk across at the car, but no one had ventured anywhere near it. Me and Paul were the first.

As we approached from the driver's side we could see that the door was tilled open and the window was smashed. Small cubes of glass lay scattered on the road beneath the tilled door. We looked through the broken window and saw blood on the driver's seat and on the fawn-coloured steering wheel, and there was a pool of blood on the floor. The passenger door was half open and the passenger seat was soaked in blood as well. There was a blood-speckled, gold cross earring lying on it, and the pearls of a broken necklace were strewn across the carpeted floor beside a woman's handbag. The blood was a thin red colour, like Raspberryade, as if someone had diluted it, but it was blood all right.

Soldiers appeared at the gate of the Mex, with their rifles pointing towards Creggan, and began making their way towards us and the long blue car. A few stayed at the gate with their rifles pointing. We retreated to the other side of the street and watched them surround the car so no one could get near it. No one spoke. The show was over. We went home.

* * *

Me and Gutsy were out the back lane behind our houses and it was pitch dark. A single streetlight stood at the bottom of the lane but its light wasn't that strong. Gunshots rang out somewhere in the near distance – single shots. We hit the deck.

'They're firing at the Mex,' said Gutsy.

A burst of quick-fire shots followed. These shots were different, louder.

'That's the BA firing back,' Gutsy told me.

I kept my head down close to the ground. I hoped there were no rats around. I hated rats. They could run over my face at this level. I could smell the dry dirt as my face was almost touching the ground. More shots rang out from the first gun, then more in return. After that it was hard to say who was shooting.

'They're firing tracers. Look,' said Gutsy and I looked up.

The bright red tracer bullets were flying through the air, moving in an arc across the sky. We couldn't see the Mex from where we were, but we could see the tracers coming from that direction.

'Tony!' I heard me da calling from the street.

'There's me da,' I said. 'I'm goney get killed for being round here at night!'

'Tony!' me da called again, this time getting closer. His repeated calls of my name could be heard over and in between the rifle and machine-gun fire.

'C'mon quick, Gutsy. Me da's calling me.'

We crawled towards the bottom of the lane where the single streetlight was; all the others had been put out weeks ago. I wasn't sure why. More shooting started, this time it was very close – probably up the top of the lane. We crawled faster and reached the bottom, then got up and ran with our heads down towards the lane opening to the street.

'Da! I'm here. You wannie see the tracers round the lane. The whole sky's lit up wi' them!'

'Tracers? I'll fuckin' tracers you! Get round to that fuckin' house!' he shouted, grabbing Gutsy and me by our collars and running us out of the lane and into the street.

As we came out of the lane, the darkened, empty street became gradually lit up by a greeny-gold colour from the sky, as if the sun has suddenly decided to shine a new colour. We all looked upwards as we ran to see a row of bright flares slowly descend from the sky ahead. We ran for our front doors. I could hear the Sixers and Pigs driving at speed on Foyle Road towards the Mex. Me da pushed Gutsy into the open door of his own house without stopping. We ran on up the street and in through our own front door. The shooting was still ringing out. It seemed to be coming from everywhere, but there were no gunmen to be seen.

When we got into the house, everyone was on the floor in the sitting room looking up towards the window. The flares still lit the sky up. All the lights in the house were out, which was normal practice by now when there was shooting at night. The smell of fear was there. Me and me da got down as well. Looking up at the window you could still see the red tracers flying across the sky. The sound of gunfire filled the room and pounded in our ears and seemed to have got even closer. No one spoke. Eventually the shooting died down until only the odd single shot could be heard in the distance. We stirred to get up.

'Stay down, stay down, it's not over!' said me da, and we all got down again on the oilcloth. I wondered how he knew when the rest of us didn't.

As I lay on the floor a glint from underneath the sofa caught my eye and I reached under and found a shilling. Saying nothing, I quietly slipped the coin into my trouser pocket. The shooting started again. This time it was in the back lane right behind our house. They were slow, aimed shots, followed by what seemed like a thousand shots in ten seconds. And then it was over. The quiet was deafening.

After a few more minutes me da said, 'It's over and it's late. Get your supper and get up to your beds.'

Me ma stood up, pulled the curtains together and put on the sitting-room light. We all rubbed our eyes, the way you do when you come out of the cinema into daylight. Supper was toast and tea as usual. We all stood around the kitchen table as there were still only two kitchen chairs. It was exciting to be getting our supper at ten at night.

All of a sudden our Paul, who was standing next to me, made a strange noise with his throat, dropped his tea on the table and fell backwards onto the kitchen floor, banging his head on the press door. The tea went all over the table and ran onto the floor.

'What in under Jesus now!' said me da in exasperation from the other end of the table.

'He's fainted, Paddy! He's fainted!' said me ma, glaring at him.

They both went to see to him on the floor. We stood and looked down at the three of them on the kitchen floor. Me ma held Paul's head up for a minute and me da held his hand, petting it. Paul woke up after a minute or two, smiled up at them and was helped to his feet. We all laughed and went to bed a few minutes later.

The next morning me and our Patrick and Paul went out into the back lane to see what we could find. Sure enough there were empty bullet shells strewn along the back lane from behind our house to the top of the lane. There were long brass shells from rifles – dozens of them. They smelled of Hallowe'en bangers. We gathered them up and took them into the kitchen to show me ma.

'Jesus, get them out of here!' she shrieked. 'We'll be jailed if the army raid the house and find them. Get them out!'

We hurriedly turned around and took them out to the back lane again, feeling a bit dejected by our ma's tone of voice. They're only bullet shells! Eventually, not wanting to ditch them altogether, we stashed them in holes in the walls that ran the length of the back lane.

While we were stashing the shells in the walls, our Patrick called us over.

'Look at that,' he said, pointing up to the bedroom window of the house next door.

There was a bullet hole in one of the panes with cracks running off it. An old couple lived there. We hardly ever saw them as they didn't go out much. I formed a picture of the oul doll lying shot dead in her bed.

'They could be shot dead in their beds,' said Patrick, echoing my thoughts.

We ran in to tell me ma, who was in the kitchen cleaning up. She told us it was all right, that our da had been speaking to them and that the bullet came in the back window, went through their bedroom wall and lodged in the front wall. 'That's why when there's shooting you get down and lie flat until it's over. No running about like a monkey, Tony Doherty!'

I ran upstairs to check my Arsenal poster on our bedroom wall. It was okay – no bullet holes in it, thank God.

Later that day I took two of the shells to the bankin', where we had made the secrets a few years earlier. Using a piece of broken glass I scraped away the grass and a half inch of soil, placed the two bullet shells together in the soil and covered them with a piece of green-coloured glass. I scraped the soil back over and patted it down with my hand. The secret was now complete.

* * *

There was a riot with soldiers from the Mex. They were out on the road behind their vehicles. The rioters were teenagers, most of them wearing jeans. We were standing at the corner watching. There was a snatch squad behind the vehicles. The squad wore white shoes of some kind – slippers or baseball boots – and carried long, white batons. They ran towards the rioters to arrest them if they could get near enough. Me ma and da must've been out because no one was sent down the street to get us.

The rioters started to get the upper hand, throwing stones and paint-bombs at the BA. Suddenly the snatch squad emerged from behind and charged at the rioters, shouting at the top of their voices. We took off up our street and stopped at our house. Some of the retreating rioters stopped at the corner and began throwing stones at the snatch squad, who had no shields on them for protection. The tables were turning. The snatch squad was exposed and hadn't caught anyone. Sensing this, we ran back down towards the corner. I lifted half a red brick as I reached the corner. There were plenty of people in front of me but I threw it anyway and hit

Davy Barbour, who was leading our younger charge, square in the back. He went down in the middle of the road in agony.

'Who the fuck threw that?' someone asked. They were lifting Davy up from the ground.

'It was Gutsy. I seen him,' I said, pointing towards the corner house, as if to say he threw and ran.

Gutsy was nowhere to be seen.

'That Gutsy's a wee fucker. Wait till I get me hands on him!' said someone else.

* * *

While we were playing football in the street, near the mound-of-soil barricade, there was the sound of gunfire in the distance. If it was far away you didn't need to hit the deck. We went on playing. The flatbed of a lorry had been deliberately parked across the end of our street. Someone had let the tyres down to make it harder to move. There was a small gap to squeeze through on our side and a bigger one on the other side. There were three barricades now in our street.

Sixers and Pigs came up Foyle Road in our direction. We stopped to look at them and gave them the fingers. They pulled up and dismounted just past the gap of Hamilton Street overlooking Anne Street, and an officer began pointing towards Creggan Hill and the cemetery. Soldiers lined up along a low wall, each on one knee, and aimed their rifles at Creggan. They looked like a row of toy soldiers. A small crowd of us children gathered behind them to see what they were going to fire at. We couldn't see anything, but the officer had a better view than us – he was looking through binoculars.

All of a sudden one soldier fired a bullet and everyone hit the deck, covering their ears. The sound was really loud.

The officer shouted at him, right into his face: 'Don't fire until I tell you! I didn't give the order!'

The soldier, a teenager, looked around at us lying on the ground. His face was blazing red with embarrassment.

Then the officer turned to us and said, 'There's going to be a lot of shooting here, so you'd better go to your houses.'

We scrambled to our feet and ran for the corner. There were about ten of us. Within a few seconds more shots rang out and we just lay in the street on our bellies until it became quiet again. It was difficult to tell if anyone was firing back at the BA, but after a few minutes the shooting died down, the soldiers got back into their Pigs and Sixers, turned on Foyle Road and drove away. There were no bullet shells for us to gather; they took them with them. We went over to the low wall and looked up the hill to see if we could see anything. There was nothing to see but houses and the speckles of black-and-white headstones in the cemetery. We went back to our football.

* * *

I awoke to the sound of heavy vehicles on the road outside.

It was summer so there was no school, and everyone else was asleep. I got up and looked out the window. There were groups of soldiers with rifles standing on the other side of the street. One of them looked up at me and gestured at me to get back into the room. I gave him the fingers and he laughed.

I got dressed and went downstairs. The front room was still in total darkness even though it was bright outside. Me da was standing at the front door looking up the street towards Melaugh's shop. There was a thick fog in the street but we could see that the soldiers had brought in a heavy crane to lift the flatbed lorry. Despite the fog it was warm and clammy and the soldiers were in their olive-green shirtsleeves under their flak jackets. There were other soldiers further up the street driving green JCBs, tackling the concrete barricade. We could hear the JCB buckets shrieking from the top of the street as they forced themselves onto the iron girders set into the concrete. A small group of soldiers were still standing across the street outside Chesty Crossan's cottage. There was no one else in the street. In the distance, you could hear the clanging of bin lids.

'The army's in, kid. No more Free Derry,' said me da, looking towards the soldiers.

He had a lit Park Drive in his hand. He drew on it and blew the smoke out. It stayed in the air in front of us for a long time.

'They're raiding rings round them. They'll be lifting everybody. Fuckers. I can't even get to me fuckin' work,' he said in frustration. 'What the fuck are you looking at, cuntyballs?' His tone of voice didn't change. I thought he was talking to me so I looked up at him in fright only to see him glaring at a soldier standing across the street, outside Chesty Crossan's door.

'You wha'?' the soldier called back.

'I said what the fuck are you looking at, cuntyballs?' said me da again.

Me da's going to get killed here, I thought. *G'won, shut your mouth, Da!* I screamed inside my head as my empty stomach felt the fear. The soldier began walking across the road towards us, lifting his rifle from his side, pointing the muzzle in our direction as he approached. Me da's breathing was getting heavy. He pulled a final drag from the Park Drive and flicked it at the approaching soldier. It whizzed past his green helmet and rolled away on the ground behind him. The trail of smoke hung in the thick, foggy air. *Thank Jesus he missed*, I said under my breath. *Da, shut up!*

'Get back in the fackin' house, Paddy!' said the soldier sharply. *How does he know me da's name?* I thought. *Is this the soldier he battered outside the Silver Dog?* The soldier was standing a yard away, at the kerb. You could see he hadn't shaved for a few days.

'You fuckin' put me in!' hissed me da, his arms folded in defiance.

I found myself standing behind him on the doorstep.

'I'll fackin' give you this!' said the soldier, bringing his rifle round to his hip. The muzzle was only a foot from me da's face. *Ah God, Da, g'won get in and close the door. He has an effin' rifle, ye know!*

'Is that right? You acting the big man with your big rifle?' said me da, smiling through his anger. 'You put that rifle down and we'll see who the big man is. Go on, put the rifle down and we'll see who the fuckin' big man is!'

Once me da's temper gets riled there's no stopping him.

The soldier stood with the rifle pointing at me da's face. Me da showed no fear of it or him. There was fear and confusion in the soldier's eyes. He was stuck.

'Put the rifle down and we'll see who the big man is,' repeated me da, putting his fisted hands on his hips and stepping down from the doorstep.

Another soldier, seeing the stalemate, approached. 'Oy, Neil, put the gun down and get back across the street!' He put his hand on Neil's shoulder to reassure him.

Me da said no more. Neil hesitated briefly, lowered the gun, turned around and walked slowly back across the street.

'Yella bastard,' hissed me da under his breath. Neil didn't hear him. We went in and closed the door.

* * *

We were all in bed on a warm evening. I woke to the sound of me ma and da arguing downstairs. Me ma was crying and she was banging doors. The front door opened and banged shut. I didn't know which one of them had left; I think it was me ma. I fell asleep thinking she was gone for ever.

* * *

The McKinneys were sent to Neilly Doherty's to get their hair cut – Terry, Michael and Dooter – so everyone else gathered to play and wait near the end of the street, not far from the barbers. You would think a bomb had hit the street! Our barricades had been taken away and all that was left were holes in the ground and deep ruts and lumps of rubber tyres left in the tar after the green army crane had dragged the long flat-bed lorry the length of the street. There was a smell of CS gas in the air, but it wasn't too bad so no one was called indoors. After a short while the three McKinneys returned from the barbers, their hair cut and flattened at the front with Neilly's lacquer.

'Baldy balls, baldy balls!' everybody shouted. 'Neilly's victims!'

The McKinneys walked with their heads down in shameful silence towards their house.

'Baldy balls, baldy balls!' we shouted as they slunk in through their front door.

The sound of a car horn filled the air from the direction of Lecky Road and got louder as it got nearer to us. Two cars were approaching at speed; one of them was a lilac-coloured

Ford Cortina with a dull black roof. The driver had his hand on the horn and we all jumped out of the way as he flew past at speed. They had to slow down a bit because of the state of the street and drove to the bottom and turned right towards the Letterkenny Road.

'There must be somebody shot over the Bog. That car is taking them up to Letterkenny Hospital,' said a man standing at his door behind us.

The other car turned around at the end of the street and drove back in the direction of the Bog. The smell of CS gas had become stronger and was starting to burn my eyes and throat.

* * *

The BA were raiding a house in our street. The Browns' house. There were no wains in it, only grown men. A crowd had gathered outside and women were banging bin lids off the ground. The noise was fierce. Young soldiers guarded the door with their SLRs. Women were spitting in the soldiers' faces and screaming at them. Then some of the women began to sing into their faces: 'Where's your mama gone?' *They're singing a pop song!* I thought. *How mad is this?*

'He has no fuckin' mammy!'

The women laughed and squealed in delight.

And then everyone started to sing, right into the soldiers' faces: 'Where's your papa gone?'

'He's no fuckin' da either!'

'Your da doesn't love ye, ya English bastard ye!'

'He doesn't know who his fuckin' da is!'

Everyone laughed hysterically again. The young soldiers' faces were red with fear and anger. They gripped their SLRs tightly and looked as if they were about to cry, or strike out.

The army came out of the house and they had one of the Browns with them by the arms – he was wearing a dark brown suit – and began marching him down the street. The women followed, pulling at the soldiers and squealing into their faces. Some of the soldiers pushed them away with their rifles, which only made the women worse. They continued towards the bottom of the street where their vehicles were. They put their prisoner in the back of a Pig, some got in beside him, and the double metal doors clanged shut. The women banged their bin lids off the side of the Pigs and Sixers. The clanging sound of metal on metal was fierce. The vehicles took off towards Craigavon Bridge, leaving the air thick with diesel fumes.

* * *

We were allowed to go to the baths in William Street in the Bog. It was a long way away from Moore Street but Terry McKinney knew how to get there and back. There was Terry, his brothers Michael and Dooter, Johnny Barbour, and me and our Paul. We all left from the street in a bunch with our trunks rolled up in a towel, clasped tightly under one arm. We also sometimes went to the baths with the school. Mr McLaughlin acted as a swimming instructor and tried to teach us how to swim.

You could smell the baths before you went through the front door. It was daylight when we went in, paid our money at the desk, went to the changing rooms, got a metal-framed basket for our clothes and got changed for the pool. Only Michael and Terry could swim, so the rest of us did dive bombs into the shallow end until we got too cold and fed up. Terry, as the oldest, agreed that it was time to go. So we all got out together, got our baskets full of clothes back and shivered in the cold changing rooms until we'd dried ourselves, and left. When we came back out it was getting dark and the streetlights were coming on. We went to the shop across the road, bunched our money together and bought Dainties, Chocolate Logs and Whoppers, which we stuffed into our mouths as we walked back from the top of the Bog towards Lecky Road.

Halfway down, Terry McKinney said, 'Wait til yis see this,' and took his wet trunks out from his damp, rolled up towel, placed the towel over his head and put the trunks over the towel. 'I'm an Arab,' he said, as he smiled and slurped on the brown Whoppers with his chocolate-stained tongue and teeth. We all did the same and in the darkening evening we all ran in a swarm like Arabs down the Bog Road making aeroplane sounds with our arms outstretched and our damp towels flapping behind us as we ran. Arab Aeroplanes was a brilliant way to travel, I thought, as we hummed and glided up the Lecky Road and onto Hamilton Street.

After a while we came back out to play football in the street. There were only a few of us and it was dark. The sound of a Sixer could be heard approaching the junction of Hamilton Street and Foyle Road. Its engine was squealing more than I've ever heard one squeal before, it was going that fast. It shot past the gap at the end of our street towards the Mex.

'Something's happened,' said Johnny Barbour. 'He's not driving at that speed for nothing.'

We returned to our football. A few minutes later we heard that a wee boy had been knocked down further up Foyle Road, towards the bridge – in Bishie country. We decided it was worth taking the chance to find out, and me, our Paul, Dooter and Johnny began walking up Bishop Street. It was getting dark.

Bishop Street had a number of terraced side streets running steeply off it down to Foyle Road. At the bottom of one of the steep streets a crowd had gathered and, as we approached, an ambulance took off in the direction of the bridge towards Altnagelvin Hospital. A woman was squealing and crying in the doorway of a house. The gathered crowd was mostly children, both younger and older than us. Most had their hands over their mouths in disbelief. Another woman had a yard brush in her hands and she was out in the middle of the road sweeping something up. It looked like a pile of jellied meat. She walked around the road from one side to the other talking to herself and crying as she pushed the heap of stuff before her with her brush.

'What's that there she's brushing?' someone asked quietly.

'That's the wee boy's guts,' replied someone else. 'The Sixer ran right over him and squashed the life out of him. He was only four or five.'

The woman continued to sweep with her yard brush, babbling and moaning and crying. A man went over to her and tried to put his arm around her, but she pushed him off and continued brushing the wee boy's guts about the road. The man went back, helpless, to the side of the road.

Someone shouted to get the wains away and we were ushered back up the street we came down. We did as we were told. When we looked back down the hill, the woman was still brushing the road, moving in and out of the shadows cast by the streetlight. The river behind her was calm, glassy and black.

When we got back down Bishop Street a crowd had gathered outside the Mex and was bombarding it with stones and bottles. We got closer to see more, but our Karen and Patrick emerged from the darkness and we were ordered home.

6

THE FOLDED NEWSPAPER

It was getting on in July 1971 and the bonfire season was approaching. Axes, hatchets and bow saws were sharpened in preparation for cutting the thick branches of the trees out the Line.

I was wearing a new mint-green wool jumper. I tore into the work with the rest of them, about a dozen boys in all, and the jumper eventually came off to reveal my white vest underneath. After we'd finished cutting and chopping I picked my new jumper up, but it caught on barbed wire. I gave it a sharp yank and, once it was free, I tied it around my waist. I positioned myself in the fork of a thick trunk of new-cut timber and began to pull it up the road towards home. The dragging leaves on the cut branches rattled noisily behind us as we hauled our bonfire fuel along Foyle Road; drivers to and from Killea had to slow down and go around us.

When we got back to Hamilton Street, I put my jumper on over my dirty vest and noticed a strand of wool sticking out from its side. I gave it a tug and made a wee hole; I pulled at it again and the gap became larger. By the time I'd reached our front door there was a sizeable gash in the jumper right across my belly. I stopped dead in my tracks and considered the consequences. Would I get thumped or would I be kept in for a week? I needed more time to think so I turned up the street towards Dooter's house.

When I reached Dooter's, Maisie, his ma, was at the door talking to another neighbour. There was a grim look of shock on her face as she dragged on an Embassy Red.

'… and killed him stone dead,' she said.

'Oh, Jesus, Mary and St Joseph, they didn't, did they?' said the other woman.

'Aye, ran right over him and left him on the road over in Westland Street. There's murder over there. All the men are out,' said Maisie.

'Oh, Jesus preserve us this day!' said the woman.

'Aye, I know,' said Maisie. 'God look to the wee boy's mother and father. We'll all be ready for Gransha if this keeps up.'

'Aye, the poor critter. We'll be ready for Gransha, surely. Our nerves will never hold out to it.'

Gransha was the local mental hospital.

Maisie looked towards me with my arm resting awkwardly across my jumper hiding the gaping hole. 'What are you hiding there, look see, young Doherty? Let me see what's up. C'mere over.' I had no choice but to drop my arm. 'Oh Jesus, Tony Doherty, your mammy's goin' to kill you!' she said, still with the fag in her mouth, and confirming for me what the likely punishment would be for destroying the new mint-green knitted jumper. 'Your mother had them knitted for yous three. You'd better get home and tell her anyway,' she said turning back towards her neighbour.

'Aye, the poor critter. Run over on the street by the army. We'll be ready for Gransha surely. Our nerves will never houl out to it.'

I headed back down the street with a heavy heart. Who would be at home – me ma or me da? What should I say? Should I cry first in the hope that I don't get thumped? Should I run away? By the time I reached the dark green door of 15 Hamilton Street I had it worked out. The front door would be open and I'd just run upstairs, take the jumper off and hide it in the press. Dead simple.

The dark green door was locked. *Oh Jesus, what will I do?* I thought. I rapped the door with the brass knocker. After a few seconds, the door opened and me ma stood waiting for me to come in.

'I've a wile sore stomach, Mammy,' I said, holding my arm across my belly as I brushed passed her and went upstairs.

'Ach son, I'll get you some Milk of Magnesia from the kitchen,' she said, appearing not to notice anything untoward.

As soon as I reached the landing the jumper came off and I stashed it at the back of the press under a pile of bedclothes. I went to our bedroom, put on a t-shirt and ran downstairs.

'I thought you said you had a sore stomach, Tony?' said me ma. 'Did you change your clothes?'

'Aye, I have, Mammy,' I said, holding my arm across my belly again. 'It started getting sore out the Line.'

'C'mon over here, son, and take some of this,' she said, clutching the big blue bottle in her hand.

* * *

The next morning me da woke me up.

'Tony, get up out of bed and come downstairs,' he said and went downstairs himself.

I realised he hadn't woken anyone else; the rest of them were still asleep in their beds.

Before I went down I noticed that the press door on the landing had been opened, but I hadn't the nerve to look in. *I'm caught here, so I am*, I thought to myself as I slowly descended. The fire was lit, despite it being summer, and had been going for a few hours. Me da was in the scullery and I eyed him through the crack in the door to see if he was in an angry mood. There was no sign of the jumper.

'How many boiled eggs do you want, Tony – one or two?' He didn't turn round from the cooker.

What's he at? I thought to myself. *If I'm caught, I'm caught. G'won, just get on with it, will ye!*

'I'll take two, Daddy,' I said and sat down at the table already set with a cup, a plate and a spoon. We had only recently got two chairs for the kitchen table, so it was a novelty sitting down to eat.

'I hear yous were out the Line chopping for the bonfire last night,' he said.

'Aye, we were all out. We chopped a wile pile of wood and dragged it all back in the road. It was class, so it was.'

'Your mammy tells me you had a wile sore stomach when you came back in. Is that right?' he asked.

'Aye, it was wile sore, so it was, but me mammy gave me medicine and it went away. I'm good at taking medicine, aren't I, Daddy?'

'You are surely, Tony. You're good at taking your medicine and your oil.'

'Aye, I am, Daddy, so I am,' I replied, slightly worried about the 'taking your oil' bit.

When the boiled eggs were done he brought them over in their egg cups along with two rounds of warm toast.

'There you go, son. Eat up!' he said as he placed the breakfast in front of me, the egg cups held between the gold-brown fingers of his smoking hand. His fingernails were black from his work as a plumber's mate at Du Ponts. This was the first time I'd seen his face since I came downstairs and he *was* annoyed. *Had he discovered the jumper?* I wondered as I dipped my egg soldier into the perfectly cooked and salted egg. And why was everyone else still in bed and me the only one at the breakfast table?

The teapot was steaming from its long spout on the cooker. Daddy lifted it and poured tea into my cup, then his. There was a glass sugar bowl on the table. He lifted the spoon to sugar the tea.

'I don't take sugar in my tea any more, Daddy,' I said, looking up at his face. 'I gave it up for Lent this year and now I cannae stand tea wi' sugar.'

'Oh, I remember now. You'll be giving up milk in your tea next Lent, will you?' He looked at me for the first time. He didn't take sugar or milk in his tea either.

'I don't know, Daddy. I think I like the milk more than the sugar,' I replied.

With a cup of black tea in one hand and a Park Drive in the other he sat down across the table. His pale blue eyes were both searching and shifty. Something was bothering him. I said nothing more, afraid that if we talked he would eventually mention the jumper. The coals in the fire crackled and hissed, and the radio was on in the sitting room, which eased the silence.

After a while he got up and went into the sitting room. I heard the rustle of paper behind me.

'Are you finished, Tony?' he said.

'Aye, Daddy, that was great,' I replied. I knew something was up.

'C'mon in here a wee minute. I have to show you something,' he said.

Jesus, Jesus, Jesus, I'm caught! I screamed in my head.

I got up from the table and went through to the sitting room, keeping a close eye on his face. His lit Park Drive was in one hand and a newspaper, folded down to one column, in the other. *Is he goin' to whack me over the head with it? All for an oul jumper? For Jesus' sake! I should've owned up and spared myself all this carry-on!*

'I have to show you something, Tony,' he said, turning the newspaper towards me.

What's this got to do with the jumper? I wondered. I found myself staring at a boy's face, black and white, bespectacled and pious-looking. It was a picture of my classmate, Damien Harkin, from the Bog. This was his First Communion photo from a few weeks earlier.

'Do you know this wee boy, Tony?'

'Aye, Daddy, I do. That's Damien Harkin from our class. What did he do to get in the paper?' I asked, not having read the headline.

'He's dead, Tony. He was killed by a three-tonner army lorry last night in Westland Street, near his house. Did you play with him at school?'

'Aye, I hang around with him, Micky Griffiths and wee Damien Healy.'

He searched my face for a few seconds.

'We'll have to go to Mass and say a special prayer for him and his mammy, daddy, sisters and brothers. Go'n get your face washed. You've a black ring round your neck. And put on something decent – maybe your new jumper.'

I suddenly looked up at me da, but he just turned away, sat down on the sofa and began reading the newspaper. I went into the bathroom, washed my face and looked in the mirror. There were still dirt marks from the night before so I used the soap. I couldn't stretch up far enough to see the ring round my neck in the mirror. *What does dead mean? Is he in heaven already?* I thought to myself. The only deaths I knew were the fluke we caught out the Line or the rats that Dandy McKinney caught. *Damien Harkin dead! And the British Army did it!*

I mulled over this solemn departure while I got ready for Mass. We children had no one to fight with, I thought. The soldiers are all big and the odds against us would be impossible. Maybe if there was a British Army made up of children! They wouldn't stand a chance against the likes of Louis McKinney or Davy Barbour; they'd flatten the wee Limeys! I went back to the bedroom where everyone was still asleep. I quietly hunted for my Sunday clothes, slipped them on and tiptoed out of the room and went back downstairs.

'Put the fireguard on the fire, Tony,' me da called in a low pitch from upstairs.

I did as I was bid, met me da as he came downstairs and we left the house together.

We walked along Hamilton Street. There were soldiers at the foot of the street but they kept their distance. It was around nine o'clock on a hot summer morning and the streets were barely alive. Everyone's front doors were closed. The bleach-scrubbed arcs at each doorstep were lilac-white and pretty-looking in the bright sunlight.

Melaugh's shop was closed. Paddy Melaugh was the Brock Man. He collected the brock from every house in the Brandywell so that he could feed his pigs which he kept in a pen out in his back yard. Me ma kept the tin brock bucket underneath the sink in the scullery and brought the brock out to Paddy when he came round each week for it in his wee van wearing his huge blue overalls.

Paddy Melaugh was at his door and me da said hello to him, nodding his head sideways and winking at the same time. Mr Melaugh said, 'Hello, Patsy', and nodded sideways and winked back. We kept walking towards Quarry Street and past the Lourdes Hall. I practised nodding my head sideways and winking my eye at the same time as we walked. It wasn't an easy thing to do.

The Grotto next to the Lourdes Hall was resplendent in the summer sun, its whitewashed walls gleaming and its cheerful array of flowers saluting the morning. Me da glanced up at Our Lady and blessed himself without breaking his stride. I did the same. We passed the Brandywell Bar on the corner and headed towards the steep, terraced street of Hogg's Folly and the Long Tower Chapel.

When we reached Charlotte Street the smell of gas, burnt

diesel and rubber from the previous evening's riot drifted up from the Bog through the early morning heat. We crossed the road to dodge the broken glass, the bits of broken brick and the plastic tops from CS gas canisters.

The chapel was cool inside; the priest had allowed the side and back doors to remain open to create a cooling draught. We sat down in the main body of the chapel behind the front pews, with me on the inside. Me da's two muckers, Eddie Millar and Tony Callaghan, whom we'd met at the door, sat beside him. I was hoping not to be on the inside because the oak panels that ran along the walls at the end of the pews had perforated panels through which, if you looked hard and long enough, you could see the dead people.

Why did they keep the dead in dark places where people have to come and pray? Was there enough room in there for everybody? Was that where Damien Harkin was going to end up, in the dark for ever? Was that where I'd end up? How could he be dead when we were in class together only a few weeks ago? What were his ma and da goin' to do without him?

'Hi boy, stand up!' me da's quiet voice in my ear shook me out of my dark questioning. 'I didn't bring you here to sleep!'

People were looking at me. The whole chapel had been standing except for me and there was a right crowd in attendance. I stood up, red-faced.

The Mass continued and I went through the motions. But the questions wouldn't leave my head. I prayed for Damien

Harkin, for his mammy, daddy, sisters and brothers. I didn't know if he had any sisters and brothers, but the order of the day was to pray for them.

'Were you at confession this week?' me da asked as he got up.

'No, we didn't go yet. Me ma said we'd go the next night,' I replied.

'Okay, kneel you there,' he said.

Up he got with Eddie and Tony and joined the queue for Holy Communion. He walked towards the altar with his hands joined in front of him and his head down. The queue wasn't that long and after a few minutes he was at the altar. He raised his head only when the priest placed the unleavened bread on his outstretched tongue. The priest proclaimed 'Body of Christ' and me da blessed himself. As he came back to our pew, he kept his hands joined together and his eyes fixed on the floor before him, awkwardly stepping sideways to get past other communicants on their way up to the altar. He was about to sit down when he suddenly glanced at me and, with a playful wink, said, 'I'm cleansed now,' before turning back to his devotions.

When the priest finished Mass everyone stood up while he left the chapel and then began to shuffle towards the doors. Me da didn't move and neither did Eddie or Tony. When most people had left, me da put his hand in his pocket and brought out an assortment of coins.

'Take a shilling out of that,' he said, offering me his money-filled hand. 'You'll have to buy a blessed candle for your wee mucker Damien to help him on his way up to heaven. Away you go. We'll wait here for you.'

I plucked a shilling out of his hand and moved across the pew past him, Eddie and Tony.

'Daddy, I've never bought a blessed candle before,' I said. 'I don't know what to do.'

'Go'n you away up with him, Patsy. The critter has to learn,' said Eddie.

Me da made his way across the pew and grabbed my hand. We walked up the central aisle of the chapel towards the altar where he opened the ornate brass gate and silently led me from the off-white marble steps to the lit-candle display to the left.

'What's the shilling for, Daddy?' I asked.

'You pay for your candles, son. Put your money in the box there in front of you,' he said, pointing to the slot in the brass plate. The shilling jangled against other coins as it fell through the slot.

'The candles are there in the wee hatch,' he said, pointing to them.

I slipped my hand into the hatch and lifted out a white candle, held it over a lit candle until it caught and pushed it into an empty slot. Following me da's lead, I blessed myself and knelt down beside him before the bright candle display.

After a minute, we made our way back from the altar to the front row, where Eddie and Tony were sitting.

We came back out again into the sunshine and made our way back down the Folly. 'Them English Bs flattened that wee boy last night,' said Eddie, dropping the rest of the curse word for my benefit.

'Aye, ah know,' replied me da. 'That's Eddie Harkin's young fella. I work with him at Du Ponts. He's in wee Tony's class in school,' he added, pointing towards the Long Tower Boys School, to where I was due to return in September to begin Primary 5.

'They're saying that the brakes were faulty but they took the three tonner off them and drove it up and down the street before they torched it. There was not a thing wrong with the brakes at all. The soldiers all jumped out and ran up the hill to the camp,' said Eddie.

'It's a bad time when not even the wains are safe in the streets,' said me da as the conversation stopped at the bottom of the Folly. Eddie and Tony said 'Churrio!' at the bottom of the street and on we went, past the long wall surrounding the grounds of the Christian Brothers' School on Lecky Road. As we walked, me da had to dodge branches and brambles overhanging the wall over the footpath. 'Daddy, I heard that a big rat fell from one of them branches and landed on a wee boy's head. Is that true?'

'Dunno, son. Could be.'

The serene whiteness of the Grotto stood in stark contrast with the cement grey of the school wall. As we passed the gate, me da suddenly stopped and, looking up at the statue, said, 'If you were to go to confession, Tony, what would you tell the priest?'

'I don't know, Daddy, ahmmmm …' Usually by the time you reached the confessional door, you'd have your list of sins ready to rhyme off: I stole sweets from my sister; I busted Dooter McKinney's ball for badness; I thumped Gutsy McGonagle for calling me names …

Me da was looking down at me. I looked up into me da's moustachioed face and with no time to think of a list said, 'I took God's name in vain last night, but only into meself, and this morning I had hatred in my heart for the soldiers who killed Damien Harkin. That's wrong isn't it, Daddy?'

'It is, son. Hatred eats at your heart. Wee Damien's death is a terrible thing, but hatred isn't goin' to bring him back. You have to pray for him just. That's all you do.' He paused for a second, thinking what to say next and said, 'So what's this about taking God's name in vain last night? What happened – did you hurt yourself out the Line or what?' He had a twinkle in his eyes and a smile twitched at the corners of his mouth.

'I tore me new jumper. I didn't mean to, Daddy. I took God's name in vain when I thought I was goin' to get caught.' It all came out in a rush. 'Am I goin' to get kept in, Daddy?'

'We know about the new jumper, Tony,' he said, taking

my hands in his and getting down on his hunkers to my level. 'Your mammy found it last night stashed in the press upstairs. But you've enough going on in your head at the minute. Forget about the oul jumper.'

And with that we walked on in the mid-morning sun, small hand in huge hand, back past Quarry Street and along Hamilton Street towards our green door, No. 15.

7

ELVIS

Me da bought Karen an Elvis poster for the bedroom wall after she sat the 11-plus exam. It was October 1971. It cost him twelve shillings and he had to save up for it for a few months, he told us later. The poster wasn't of the young, thin Elvis with the lacquered quiff; it showed the more mature, round-faced, long-sideburns version, though he still had pearly-white teeth and wore a denim shirt. His head was huge and filled most of the poster, though it went down as far as his dark chest hair, where a gold medallion nestled. Elvis went up on the bedroom wall. I had to move my Arsenal team poster to the right to make room, Charlie George and all.

You could see Elvis' teeth from Chesty Crossan's front door on the other side of the street if you looked up at our window. I had to tell everyone it wasn't mine in case they thought I was into Elvis. When the bedroom light was on you could see his whole head. When it was off and the curtains were open, the streetlight made his teeth stand out.

A few days after her exam Karen looked up from Chesty's

front door at Elvis on our bedroom wall. Elvis was missing a tooth! His other teeth were fine, though, and gleamed as normal.

She rushed into the house, the three of us following. We all stood facing the poster in the bedroom. One of his teeth had been coloured in with a blue pen. None of us was to blame. By the look of Patrick and Paul it wasn't them; it wasn't me either. Her Elvis was dead to her – destroyed. There was no sign of a murder weapon. Karen cried her eyes out with her hands up to her face. She was a wild crier when she started.

'Daddy'll be home from work shortly. He'll sort yous out,' she said between sniffles. 'How could yous do that to me?'

She lined us up in the bedroom and scanned our faces for clues – a flicker of guilt or a smirk. Eventually the identity parade was allowed to stand down and we went off to watch *Blue Peter* on TV.

'Should be "Blue Elvis",' our Patrick whispered in my ear.

We giggled. So did Paul, though he hadn't heard what Patrick said. Karen sat in the chair opposite and cried her way through the programme. Every few minutes she glared at us from her chair as if she could squeeze the truth out of us with her eyes. This was great craic, as it wasn't me – definitely not, and definitely a mystery. She wasn't that mad about Elvis or anything like that so I couldn't see why she was that bothered.

As six o'clock drew nearer and we waited for me da to come home, the crisis deepened. Any cockiness among us had reduced to nervous cackling. Me da hadn't been himself recently, and him and me ma were rowing all the time, mostly when we were in bed. You could hear the tone of the argument but only some of the words. Doors banged and me ma cried. I lay in bed at night worrying that one of them wouldn't be there in the morning when we got up.

As soon as Karen heard me da coming in through the front door she ran out to the hall and turned on the crying again.

'Daddy, wan of themuns coloured in Elvis' tooth!' she bawled. 'He's destroyed, Daddy, so he is. He's destroyed.'

The three of us had squeezed into the far corner of the sofa away from the door when me da had come in. When he came through the door his jaw dropped and the fury rose immediately on his face. *Aw, Jesus*, I thought to myself, *here we go*.

'Right, the three of yis. Up the fuckin' stairs! Get up them stairs!' he roared, as he took off his coat and let it fall to the floor.

Paul was the first through the door to the stairs and got a sharp crack on the backside on the way past, which helped him up the first few.

'Yous two, get up there now!'

Me and Patrick paired up and made a break for the door, but he caught both of us with a crack on the ear and slapped the arses off us as we scrambled up the stairs in panic, getting in each other's way.

We were made to stand with our backs to the poster and facing the bedroom window. Me da pulled the curtains because a group of wee girls had gathered across the street out of sympathy for Elvis' tooth and Karen's loss. She stood at the door and watched.

'Right, I want the truth. Which one of ye did it?' me da roared into our faces. The wee girls across the street had no picture but plenty of sound. 'Which one of ye? Yis better own up or it's a hammering for the three of ye,' he bellowed.

We knew that without needing to be told. But it wasn't me so I was saying nothing. *God wouldn't forgive him for thumping me, an innocent boy*, I thought.

'Turn around! Turn around!' he snapped at us.

We all turned around quickly on his command. He was behind us and everyone was facing the dead Elvis. The blue tooth that killed him was in the very centre of the poster, just above our heads. It didn't look that bad, I thought. Me da grabbed Patrick by the shoulders and turned him back round to face him. Oldest first.

'Tell me the truth or ye know what's goin' to happen, don't you, boy?' His voice was calmer but somehow more menacing. This wasn't good.

'It wasn't me, Daddy. I like Elvis, so I do,' he pleaded.

Both me and Paul sniggered, more out of nerves than anything else.

'Yous boys shut up! I'll give yis somethin' to laugh about

in a minute!' he said and slapped the legs off Patrick who was in tears.

'I didn't do it, Daddy. It must've been wan of them two,' bawled Patrick.

Me da grabbed him by the shoulders and quarter-turned him to face the holy picture on the other wall.

'Swear to me now in front of that picture that it wasn't you!' he demanded.

Our Lord stared back with mercy and forgiveness in his eyes, his bloody hands open, forgiving. Our Lord wasn't our da, unfortunately.

'I swear to God, Daddy, it wasn't me,' Patrick cried, rubbing the redness on his calves with one hand and his red ear with the other.

With that, me da swung him around again to face Elvis along with me and Paul. Paul was crying hard and shaking by this time.

'You, boy, turn around,' he snapped and turned me around. The second oldest boy. We always got it in sequence.

'You saw what your brother got. D'ye want the same, d'ye?'

'Naw, Daddy, but it wasn't me. I didn't colour him in. I was out playin' when I came back from school.'

Having an alibi was no good. He was determined and on a roll. He slapped our legs or arses each time he asked one of us a question. I too was brought in front of Our Lord.

'Swear over the Sacred Heart! Tell the truth!' he hissed, no longer shouting.

The Sacred Heart was a real heart in Our Lord's open chest.

'I swear over the Sacred Heart that it wasn't me. I didn't do it. I dunno who did it, Daddy,' I sobbed, rubbing my stinging arse.

I looked into Our Lord's eyes for the truth and found only pain. Me da swung me back round to face Elvis. Then he moved on to Paul, the youngest.

'Daddy, it's all right. It doesn't matter. I can get another one,' pleaded Karen on our behalf, belatedly realising the horror she'd unleashed.

'Naw, ye cannae. D'ye think twelve shillings will grow on a tree out the Daisy Field, d'ye?' he roared in response.

She said nothing. There was no point. He grabbed Paul, turned him around and began the process of truth-seeking with him, slaps and all. They were lighter though – you could tell by the sound. Paul cried the hardest all the same and snivelled uncontrollably, barely able to swear in front of the holy picture that it wasn't him. The interrogation had drawn a blank. Me da was very unhappy.

'Right, get your clothes off and into bed!' he roared, pointing to the beds. 'There'll be no tea for yous the night. Fuckin' cowboys, that's what yis are!'

We quickly removed our clothes, revealing the full array of red patches on our legs and arses. Soon, all that could be seen were our heads, our red ears all the more noticeable on the white pillows. Bright autumn sunlight streamed through the orange curtains. The door was closed and we were left alone in our suffering.

As me da shut the door he added, 'Not wan of yis better get out of that bed. I'll be listening out. If I hear any nonsense I'll be up wi' the belt!'

Being in bed without our tea and in pain was one thing, but what made the situation worse was that we could hear every wain in the street out playing below our window, and we knew that at least two of us were innocent.

'Which one of you two bastards did it?' whispered Patrick from his side of the bed after we heard the sitting-room door closing. 'It was you Tony, wasn't it?'

'Naw, it wasn't me, Pansy Potter,' I said in a girl's voice, mocking him. 'I'm telling me da that you said a curse. Look at the state of ye – your ear's purple! Haha!'

After a few minutes of silence, broken only by the occasional snivel, I turned to Paul and said, 'I bet ye it was this wee shite here.' I pointed a finger into Paul's snottery face lying beside me.

He was crying silent tears and barely able to communicate. 'N-n-n-naw. I d-d-d-didn't d-d-o it,' he cried and turned his face to the wall.

'Ye wee liar, ye!' I said and swung my leg at him under the blankets. I hit him in the thigh with my knee.

The springs of the bed shook and rattled. We heard the sitting-room door open downstairs and lay stock still.

'I'll be up if I hear another thing!' roared me da from the hall, closing the door again with a bang.

We all let out a sigh of relief. That was close!

Elvis was still on the wall. So was Arsenal. No one had coloured Arsenal in. I scanned the team above my head and guessed who they were from my upside-down position. Charlie George was my favourite. Then there was George Graham and Pat Rice, who I liked because he was Irish; Bob Wilson, the keeper with his friendly face and curly hair; Peter Storey, Frank McLintock, the captain, and George Armstrong. I was converted to Arsenal from Man United after seeing Charlie George score his screamer in the FA Cup Final against Liverpool in May. He lay on the pitch in the sun after scoring it and his teammates had to lift him up. His long hair trailed behind him as he ran and he talked the same way as the English soldiers at the Mex army post.

Paul fell asleep. It was dark outside and the whole street was still out playing – tig by the sound of it.

Patrick was sitting up. 'I heard me da goin' out,' he said and got out of bed.

He went to the window and peeped around the curtains. I followed, feeling safe knowing that me da was out and the two of us stood there in our white vests and underpants with our heads poking through the curtains. Only a few street lamps were lit and all the wains were playing under a lamp post across from us. Someone saw us and pointed up. It was Jacqueline McKinney. We brought our heads back in quickly, affronted to be in bed when everyone else was out. But a wee minute later we poked our heads through again – we couldn't help ourselves.

'El-vis! El-vis! El-vis! El-vis!' they all chanted as soon as they saw us at the window.

'Fucking bastards!' shouted Patrick, quickly snapping the curtains shut again. He didn't care about cursing. After a minute or two I poked my head through the curtains again.

'El-vis! El-vis! El-vis! El-vis!'

I snapped the orange curtains closed and jumped back.

'Get into bed, ya eejit, ye!' said Patrick, who was back in bed again. 'You got us into this shite in the first place. G'won, admit it. I'll call me ma up and you can tell her. Me ma won't hit ye.'

'It wasn't me, Patrick. I think it was him.' I pointed at Paul, who was still asleep.

'For fuck's sake,' was all Patrick said.

We fell asleep licking our wounds and feeling sorry for ourselves. At least two of us were hard done by. When we got up in the morning, Elvis was gone. Arsenal were on their own again up on the bedroom wall.

8

THE RICKETY WHEEL

In early December 1971 the first Christmas tree of the season appeared in the front room of a house further up Hamilton Street, just opposite Paddy Melaugh's shop. I was on my way home from school, it was almost dark, with a looming grey sky, and the streetlights hadn't yet come on, and I saw its coloured lights flickering on and off as I passed the shop. The pretty lights glittered in the window, taunting me, and I stopped to look. There was a woman standing behind the tree and she saw me. I set off towards No. 15, checking for more flashing lights and other tinselly signs of Christmas as I went. But there was nothing – at least, there was nothing obvious. Maybe families had their trees, lights and decorations up in their sitting rooms, where they couldn't be seen from the street. I was bothered that we weren't the first in the street to have our decorations up, but I quietly panicked when I thought that we might be the last.

When I reached the house the front door was closed. That meant there was no one in and I was the first home from school. I stood on the doorstep in the cold with my hands in the pockets of my dark blue duffle coat with its yellow-coloured wooden buttons. I scanned the line of cottages and houses opposite ours to check for any signs of Christmas decorations. Lena Carlin, our next-door neighbour, turned the corner at the bottom of the street. She was on her way home from work. Lena lived with her brother and Hugh, her husband.

'You locked out, Tony?' she asked as she put her key in the door.

'Aye, Lena, but I'm all right here.'

'You must be foundered. D'ye not want to come in until somebody comes wi' a key?' she asked.

'Naw, Lena. I'm okay.'

'C'mon in o' that. You're blue wi' cold.' She smiled and held the door open.

I went in after her and she closed the front door.

'C'mon in to the heat,' she said as she led me into the sitting room.

Her brother, Séamus, was lying on the dull-brown leather sofa with a purple woollen blanket over him. He muttered a hello as we came in. He had the same dark copper hair as Lena and was wearing a grey and white striped shirt that could have been a pyjama top.

'He's wild sick,' she said looking at him and then at me.

I didn't say anything. On the floor beside the sofa was a tin bucket that had dark-coloured liquid at the bottom. He was a wild pale colour and his lips were ruby red.

'I have to go to the shop for spuds. Hugh'll be in shortly from his work,' she called from the kitchen. 'Will you watch him til I come back?'

Jesus, I thought, *what if he throws up and dies and me on my own?* 'Aye, okay, Lena,' I replied, a bit unsure of myself.

'Are you sure, Tony? I'll only be a wee minute,' she said, walking through the sitting room and out into the hall without stopping. She was out the front door without waiting for my answer.

I sat opposite Séamus and watched him as he lay staring up at the ceiling. He looked at me and I turned away towards the fire, which needed more coal and a good poke. It was warm enough, though, which was comforting. All of a sudden he made a noise in his throat and sat up with a start, swung his head over the side of the sofa and heaved a reddy-brown liquid from his mouth with a load groan, as if his tongue was trying to escape. He retched again but nothing came out this time, just noises.

Jesus Christ! I thought, gripping the arms of the armchair. *He's goney die and me here on my own!* He stayed in his vomiting position, making more groaning noises as dark brown slabbers hung from his mouth. I was glued to my chair with fear, my heart going like mad, afraid to say anything in case I brought on his death. *Jesus, Lena, come back quick!* I thought.

Is that blood he's throwin' up or what? I wondered, having

193

never seen such a sight before. We stayed in our positions, him half-hanging off the sofa and me stuck to the matching chair. The only sound in the room was his stomach heaving and gurgling, his heavy breathing and the odd groan. Just then I heard the front door; then the vestibule door opened and Lena came back in with a small brown paper bag of spuds in her arms. I hadn't realised I'd been holding my breath until I let it go as she came in through the sitting-room door.

'Was he throwing up again, the poor critter?' she asked as he put his head back down on the pillow. There were beads of sweat on his forehead.

Séamus nodded, and wiped his mouth and chin with his stripy sleeve.

'He's a wile sickness on him, the critter. He's been lyin' for days wi' it.' She had her purse in her hand, which she opened and took out a two-bob coin.

'Here's something for you, Tony,' she said, offering me the money. 'It'll not be long till it's time for the Rickety Wheel. Keep you this two bob for it.'

'Ach, naw, Lena. You're okay,' I said, half-heartedly, hoping for a second offer.

'Ach, away o' that wi' you.'

'Thanks, Lena,' I said as she put the silver coin in my outstretched hand.

'There's someone in your house now. I saw the door open. You can go on in.'

'Thanks, Lena,' I said, realising that my voice was a bit shaky. When I got up I couldn't help looking into the tin bucket again to see the dark red-brown stuff at the bottom with some splashed on its sides. 'Churrio! See yis later.'

'Churrio, son!' said Lena.

I opened the sitting room door and closed it behind me. *The Rickety Wheel!* I thought to myself as I hit the cold air outside. I rubbed the two-shilling coin in my trouser pocket. *The Rickety Wheel! I cannae wait!*

* * *

Over the next few days more Christmas lights appeared in other windows. A few times we took the chance and came down Bishop Street through Bishie country. Nearly all the houses in Sunbeam Terrace, opposite Nazareth House, had Christmas trees in their bay windows. One would be all coloured lights, the next would be white, the next would have flashing coloured lights. Patrick, Paul and I gawked into each of them as we passed until the terrace gave way to the high College wall. This was the dangerous part, as the worst of the Bishies usually hung around here. But our luck was in.

One day, as we were about to get out of the classroom to go home, a loud gunshot rang out somewhere nearby. We all hit the floor, teacher and all. A few more shots rang out and then there was silence.

'Stay down till I tell yous to get up,' the teacher said. It was

Mr McCartney. Mr McCartney had a mass of sandy hair, a bushy moustache and sideburns covering most of his face. Everyone in the class liked him, not just because he looked different from the other men teachers, who mostly had short back and sides like us, but because he was really dead on.

No one moved for about five minutes. There wasn't a sound outside in the corridors. Inside, some of the boys were giggling after someone let out a loud fart. Mr McCartney laughed too as he lay with his face on the wooden floor. A few doors could be heard opening out in the corridor and we could hear whispered voices.

'Okay, up yis get, boys,' said Mr McCartney.

After we got up and dusted down our coats and trousers we were warned not to go down Bishop Street, for someone had been shot and there was a chance that another gun battle might start. We went down the Folly, and the boys from Bishop Street and Abercorn Road were kept in.

The next morning, me, Patrick and Paul came up Bishop Street towards school. We'd heard that a soldier had been shot at the side of Grant's shop and that the gunman had shot him from the College wall. We crossed the road towards Grant's. There was a small pool of blood on the ground where the soldier had been shot. It had frozen over. There were other boys and girls there, but no one touched the frozen blood. We all stepped round it. It was probably bad luck to step on it – like stepping on someone's grave in the cemetery.

As we turned to go on to school I noticed a small, round hole in the red brickwork just above the frozen pool of blood. It was about a foot from the ground. *The soldier must've been shot in the leg and the bullet went right through*, I thought as I got down on my hunkers and stuck my little finger in the hole. It went in the whole way. As I poked around I felt something sharp and pulled my finger out again to see if it was cut.

'There's something inside the hole,' I said to Patrick and Paul.

I stuck my finger in again and poked about until I was able to get the thing moving. Eventually I poked it out of the hole and into the palm of my hand.

'Jesus, look at this, hi!' I said excitedly as I stood up.

It was a bullet head – a shiny brass bullet head that still had blood on it. Other boys hanging out at the shop crowded around wide-eyed to see what it was and made whistling noises of disbelief. I kept it clutched in my hand and we took off up Bishop Street with a posse of school wains in tow.

We went in through the school gate on upper Bishop Street and walked in a crowd towards the playground where the whole school of several hundred boys were running around with their coats on to keep warm. Mr McCartney and Mr O'Kane saw us coming. I could tell by looking at them that they knew something was afoot. I made towards them and the crowd followed.

'Look what I got, Mr McCartney,' I said, my hand out-stretched. I had an audience surrounding me.

'What is it, Tony?' he asked, looking a bit worried and puzzled.

'It's a bullet head, sir,' I said. 'It's from the soldier who was shot yesterday in Bishop Street. It went right through his leg. It still has his blood on it. Look!'

Mr McCartney and Mr O'Kane exchanged grim looks.

'Here, just give it to me, Tony. I'll take care of it,' Mr Mc-Cartney said, holding his hand out under mine. I tipped the bullet head into his hand.

'Did the soldier die, sir?' asked someone behind me. 'Was he shot dead, sir?'

'No, he wasn't,' said Mr McCartney, looking over our heads towards the school doors. 'Now, away now and play yourselves! The bell's goney be rung any minute now.'

* * *

Although our street had become a very different place in the space of a year, with shooting, rioting and army raids, us wains all still had to be good for Santa, just like any other year. One day, when we got home, me ma and da had the decorations out of the press and had them laid out in their open tins on the sofa. At last! The sight sent a shiver of excitement through us children and we all hovered and buzzed about the sitting room like bluebottles in high summer.

We used the same decorations as we had in Moore Street. Me da didn't like putting them up too early in December and we were usually the last in the street, by a day or two, to put them up. It was usually around the fifteenth. Everyone else in my class had theirs up already and it was the whole talk of the class. I just had to pretend that ours were up too, rather than be affronted or left out. But now they were going up for real I didn't need to keep the lie going.

The decorations were kept in several Rover biscuit tins out of harm's way – one for the shiny balls, one was for tinsel, one for the Christmas tree lights, and one for the decorations themselves. Every year when we opened the tins there were usually a few shiny balls broken, which might or might not be replaced depending on how many intact ones there were left. The Christmas tree lights rolled up from last year wouldn't work and needed new bulbs; the paper decorations needed Sellotaping here and there.

The decorations were thin strips of pastel-coloured paper, which we usually pinned into the four corners of the living room ceiling and looped into the centre above the suspended light. The same pattern was repeated from the middle of the walls at the ceiling and looped in towards the light. Me ma and da were up on a chair each in the living room making the loops and I was in charge of handing up the drawing pins.

'You're goin' to like what Santa's bringing you this year, Tony,' said me da, taking a pin from my outstretched hand.

'Is that right, Da? What is it?'

'Shut up, Paddy,' said me ma up on her chair. 'No talk about what Santa's bringing. He brings what he brings. They've all been good. And you' – she glared down at me from way up high – 'your daddy's your daddy, not Da!'

The other wains were fluttering around all excited, doing this and that to both help and hinder.

'What am I gettin', Daddy?' asked our Patrick, careful to address him correctly.

'What about me, Daddy?' said Paul, taking his cue from Patrick.

Me da, under a glare from me ma, just said, 'Ach, yous'll all see, if yous are good,' and that was the end of the in-quisition.

The tinsel Christmas tree was placed near the window beside the TV. We had to move a chair to the front room to make way for it. Once the bulbs were all screwed tight and the broken ones replaced, the lights were plugged in, instantly releasing the true magic of Christmas. We had two sets of lights, one bright white and the other coloured. Me da looped them around the tree from the bottom up until they tapered out near the angel at the top. The shiny balls, all fantastic colours of purple and red and orange, as well as gold and silver, were hung from their small wire hoops on the ends of the silver branches.

The final part of the sitting room's transformation was

the removal of the everyday ornaments from the fireplace to make way for Christmas cards and strips of tinsel.

Christmas was finally on its way to the Doherty house!

* * *

The whole family gathered after tea. Six wains (we now had another addition to the family, Glenn, who was still just a baby) and me ma and da. We were heading to the Rickety Wheel in the Lourdes Hall. Everybody in the street was going, it appeared – at least, all the families with wains were going – and so were the families from Quarry Street, Anne Street, Lecky Road, Brandywell Road and Southend Park, as well as Deanery Street and Donegall Place. At the front door there was a logjam of people, while prams, some of them huge, had to be carted up the stone steps.

The Lourdes Hall itself was a huge tin hut with a red-brick front, lodged between Quarry Street and the Grotto. We played indoor football in it sometimes with the school, when we'd walk down the Folly in a long line, hand-in-hand with another boy in the class and teachers – usually Mr O'Kane and Mr McCartney – at the front and the back to keep watch. Inside, the hall was teeming with people. Wains in prams were squealing or just sitting up looking out in wonder while older people sat in chairs in the middle and back of the hall. Everyone else stood round the stage up at the front where the Rickety Wheel was. A haze of smoke filled the hall, and people flashed around the fags – Embassy Red, Number Six, Sovereign and Park Drive – as they stood around in groups talking, waiting for the MC to come up on stage and get the whole thing going. Me da stood over to the side of the hall with a group of other men, all smoking their Park Drives. There was a stall beside them selling bottles of minerals and crisps.

The Rickety Wheel was a huge circular board painted white with numbers in black at regular intervals around the edge and a nail hammered into the outside edge of the board next to each number. A piece of flexible metal was attached to the top of the board, which made a ratcheting noise as it flipped past each numbered nail on its way round.

At the front of the stage, almost within touching distance on the other side of a low wooden picket fence with a gate in the middle, were the prizes: a green plastic American army tank still in its box that had a see-through plastic front; Gola football boots of various sizes; a Celtic rig and a Man United rig; a cowboy cap gun, still in its box, with a wee packet of caps taped to it; a number of 1971 *Shoot* annuals with a cover picture of Alan Ball and Bobby Moore; Selection Boxes and Christmas stockings bunged with sweets and chocolate; tins of Roses and Quality Street; tins of Rover biscuits; bottles of sherry; Christmas cakes with white icing and holly leaves; fruit cakes and cherry cakes. There were things for girls as well.

Paddy Melaugh, the MC, got up on the stage to take control. Before announcing the start of proceedings, he checked the Rickety Wheel from behind and, without a word, sent it spinning for a test run. Away it went, releasing its magical rickety-rickety clickety-clickety sound and brought the whole hall to attention. As the wheel slowed down he spun it again and the noise filled the smoky hall. Then Paddy lifted the microphone from a chair on the stage.

'Ladies and gentlemen, good people of the Brandywell,' he boomed out round the hall, 'you're all welcome to the Lourdes Hall. This is the moment all yous wains have been waiting for. Isn't that right, wains?'

'Aye!' all the wains squealed up to him.

'I didn't hear ye's. I said isn't that right, wains?' He cupped one ear with his hand.

'Aye!' we all shouted at the tops of our voices. The wains in the prams started crying and some of the mas had to go to them at the back of the hall.

'Right now, everybody. Get your tickets here at the front. This run is a white ticket. Let's go! The quicker you get your tickets, the quicker the show starts and the Rickety Wheel goes round!'

People queued with their money in clenched hands at the foot of the stage to buy their tickets – big people and children. Me ma gave each of us a shilling. A shilling was by then worth five pence in the new decimal money. I couldn't make my mind up if I should spend some now or wait until later. I still had the two bob that Lena Carlin gave me when I was in her house. I'd stashed it behind a piece of loose wallpaper near the skirting board below our bed and hadn't told anyone about it.

Paul and Patrick joined the queue. I stayed where I was and kept my hand round the two coins inside my trouser pocket. Once they'd bought their tickets they came back to where we all stood. We were together except for Glenn, our newest brother, who was sitting up at the back of the hall, his bald head protruding from the pram. We waved back at him every once in a while and he'd smile back at us through the haze.

'What did you get?' me ma asked them.

'I got 25, 26 and 27,' said Patrick. 'Ye get three for a shilling.'

'And I got 28, 29 and 30,' said Paul, showing her the tickets in his hand.

When all the tickets were sold Paddy took the mic again. 'Okay, ladies and gentlemen. Here we go for the first turn of the Rickety Wheel for 1971! After three, everybody.'

'ONE! ... TWO! ... THREE!' the hall shouted in unison and Paddy spun the wheel to start the rickety-clickety sound for real. Round and round it went, the noise filling the hall. All eyes were on the wheel as the sprung metal flipped past each nail, quickly at first and then slowing down until it drew to a breath-stopping halt.

'Number twenty-five! Who has number twenty-five?' called Paddy from the stage.

Patrick was dumbstruck. His mouth hung open and he just stood and gawked at me ma.

'Number twenty-five. Who has it?' Paddy boomed out.

'Jesus, here Paddy!' said me ma and, swooping the ticket from Patrick's hands, went towards the wee gate to be let through by the man on the other side. Patrick followed after her, a big smile on his face.

'Now, Eileen, what are you going to take with you? The choice is yours,' said Paddy on the mic as she walked the length of the row of prizes. She lifted a tin of Rover biscuits and held them up for Paddy to see. 'Oh, a tin of Rover! Well done, Eileen and wee Doherty. We'll all be over on Christmas Day for a sup o' tea!'

Everyone laughed, and me ma and Patrick came back out through the gate.

'And now we're going to do a freeeeeeee run! Hold on to your tickets as we're doing a freeeeeeee run!' announced Paddy.

The whole hall immediately looked at the floor, scrambling to find the tickets they'd rolled up and tossed away. Paddy spun the Rickety Wheel and round it went, all eyes glued to it. And it clicked round and round, slowed to an uncertain stop with the sprung metal balancing on a nail – and then it fell back.

'Number sixty-three! Who has number sixty-three?' Paddy called out.

'Here, Paddy!' cried a voice from behind us.

I knew the voice. It was Gutsy's ma, and sure enough, up she came to the stage in her dark brown coat and orange headscarf with her ticket in her hand. She was let through the gate and emerged shortly after with a large white iced cake with shiny green holly on it in a see-through box. She was smiling from ear to ear.

'Okay, Mrs McGonagle. I'll be over to you after visiting the Dohertys on Christmas Day. Hamilton Street is hacking up the night.'

Everyone from our street roared and laughed in approval; everyone else smiled and booed and shouted 'Fix!' and 'Fraud!'

After a few more spins of the Rickety Wheel I took my chance and queued for tickets. I bought three with the shilling me ma had given me and kept the two bob coin in my pocket. I got numbers 45, 46 and 47. I stood with the rest of them waiting for the next spin of the wheel.

Round and round went the Rickety Wheel. It took ages to slow down and eventually stop.

'Sixty-seven. Who has number sixty-seven?' called Paddy from the stage and a woman from the back of the hall came forward to claim her prize.

I kept a grip on my three tickets in case there was a free run. But Paddy didn't announce it after they let the woman back out through the wee gate. He just called on people to buy their tickets for the next spin of the wheel.

Towards the end of the first night of the Rickety Wheel I still had the two bob coin in my trouser pocket, wondering if I could sneak up and buy more tickets without anyone seeing me. As I fingered the coin in my pocket Paddy called out from the stage: 'The next spin of the Rickety Wheel is for the special mystery prizes. Come on and get your tickets!'

The hall hummed with word of the special prizes, and women fumbled in their purses and headed for the ticket-seller. I took my hand out of my pocket for the fiftieth time that evening and the two bob coin came out with it and hit the wooden floor with a clatter. My heart sank as I watched it roll and fall over in surrender between me ma's feet.

'Where did you get that, Tony?' she asked, bending down to pick it up.

'Lena gave it to me one day when I was locked out,' I replied.

'They've called for the special prizes. Here – take you that and queue up for tickets,' she said, handing the coin back to me.

'What's the special prizes?' I asked her.

'Ach, you don't know until you get them,' she said with a smile, and she looked away towards the stage. 'Away you go!'

As I joined the back of the queue I imagined what the special prizes would be. The *Shoot* annual with the cowboy cap gun? The American army tank with the Gola football boots? I just didn't know. For my two bob I got six pink tickets numbered 101, 102, 103, 104, 105 and 106 and walked back to where we were gathered in the hall. Me da was there as well now, fiddling with his black Mexican-style moustache and looking around him.

'What did you get, Tony?' he asked.

'One-oh-one to one-oh-six,' I said, holding the tickets up.

'Your ma told me that Lena gave you two bob. What was that for?' he asked.

'I don't know, Da. She just gave it to me when I was locked out of the house one day a wee while ago.'

'God, aren't you the boy!' he said with a smile, rubbing my head with his hand.

'Okay, ladies and gentlemen of the Brandywell!' said Paddy through the mic. 'We're goin' to spin the Rickety Wheel for the special prizes! Let's go! And hold on to your tickets after this spin for a freeeeeeeeee run!'

He turned and grabbed the edge of the wheel and gave it an almighty tug. Around it spun and spun and spun … and spun more slowly until it settled on a number.

'One-oh-three! Who has a hundred and three?'

That was me! I'd won! Like Patrick I was stunned into silence and could only hold the tickets up for me ma and da to see.

'Here, Paddy! We won!' me ma called up.

'Dear God, bless us and save us! It's Eileen Doherty from Hamilton Street again! C'mon up, Eileen!' called Paddy.

Yes! I said to myself as me ma took me by the ticket hand and led me towards the stage. The cowboy cap gun was still on the stage and the Gola boots were there as well. *I hope they have my size!* I thought as the gate was opened.

'Hello, Eileen,' said Paddy, bending down to speak to her. 'It's a turkey or a ham, as usual.' He pushed his thick black-rimmed glasses up his nose. No one paid the least bit of attention to me, the winner with the winning ticket gripped in my hand. 'Which do you want?' he asked her.

'Aw, I'll take the turkey, Paddy,' she replied with a satisfied grin.

'That's grand, Eileen. I'll bring it over on Christmas Eve. Fresh as the day it was born!'

'Dead on, Paddy. We'll be stuffed the year!' she said, and both of them gave a hearty laugh.

I wanted to cry. *How could she do that to me?* I asked myself in self-pity as we turned to go back out through the wee gate. I gave a last glance at the cowboy cap gun, the Gola football boots and the American army tank as I dragged my heels after me ma back towards my family gathered in the centre of the hall.

'Hi, Paddy. Look at thon,' said me ma to me da, presenting me by the hand. 'He has a face on him.'

I looked up at them looking down at me and looked to the

ground. I couldn't hide my sadness and disappointment. My face said it all.

'What's wrong wi' you, boy?' asked me da.

As if you don't effing know! I said in my head, still looking away from them.

'Didn't ye win us a turkey for the house at Christmas?' he said, holding my chin up with his smoky fingers.

'I know I did … but I wanted the cowboy cap gun and a pair of football boots. They're Golas! All we got is an oul shite turkey!'

'Sure aren't we goin' to get you …' Me ma's sentence stopped abruptly and her and me da looked at each other.

'Sure ye never know what Santa's goin' to bring you, son,' said me da, rubbing my head again as we headed for the door of the hall to go home. 'Ye just never know.'

9

THE RAY GUN

In the run-up to Christmas Day all the children in the street were beside themselves with excitement; some took sick with it. We were all Santa-believers as far as I was concerned. When me ma and da came back from the town late one afternoon shortly before Christmas, Karen ushered us all into the sitting room while ma and da went straight upstairs. You could hear the clatter and bang of bulky packages as they went up. We looked at each other in silence, wondering what they were at; they didn't normally go upstairs when they got back from the town.

'That's Mammy with our new clothes for Christmas,' said Karen, knowing what to say even though she was only eleven.

The next morning we were hanging around the house. Out of the blue, Patrick said, 'C'mon upstairs till ye's see somethin'.'

Paul and I followed him upstairs and into me ma and da's room.

'Look up there,' he said, pointing.

On top of the big press in the corner of the room were a number of large brown-paper bags with boxes sticking out

THIS MAN'S WEE BOY

of them. It was obvious it was a selection of toys and games.

'I know what you're getting for Christmas,' Patrick whispered to me.

'What do you mean? Sure only Santa and my da know. They're not for us,' I replied.

'Aye, they are. Paul, you're getting a ray gun, and you're getting cars,' he said, pointing at me.

'They're not for us, ya pansy! I'm tellin' on you when me ma and da come back from work!' I shouted and ran out.

Patrick ran after me into our room, grabbed me and pinned me to the floor with his hands on my shoulders.

'If you tell, I'm telling me da you called me a pansy and he'll kill ye!' he shouted into my face.

He was right, but he'd get killed as well for showing us the stuff.

'Okay, but they're not for us, aren't they not?'

'Naw, they're not,' he said, but I could tell by his smirk that he knew something I didn't want to know. 'But there's a tin of Quality Street there as well. I dare you to open it!'

'Naw, we'll be killed! I'm not opening it!' I said.

Karen had heard the clatter from downstairs and came up to see what was going on. Karen was mammy when me ma was out – sort of.

'What's goin' on in here?' she demanded to know.

'I told our Tony about the Quality Street, so I did,' said Patrick.

She gave him a knowing look. 'G'won down the stairs and get the Sellotape from the drawer,' she said to me.

Away down to the kitchen I went and brought the Sellotape up. Patrick reached up and lifted the Quality Street tin down from the press and proceeded to unpick the Sellotape that sealed the lid to the tin. It came off in one long, loud strip. He made a ball with it in his hand.

'It'll be okay. Me ma and da'll not know,' said Karen, as she opened the lid to reveal all the shiny, colourful, wrapped sweets, like jewels in a chest. 'We can tape it up when we're finished. It'll be okay!'

She handed me one. It was a toffee penny in a gold wrapper. It was rock-hard at first with the cold in the room, but it soon softened in the heat of my watery mouth. I took more toffee pennies and they took some sweets too. We put the wrappers back in the tin so as not to make a mess. Then Karen wrapped the Sellotape around the lid to re-seal it and placed it back up on top of the press.

On Christmas Eve we had our bath as if it was Saturday night. Us three boys had all been sent to the barbers that morning for short back and sides. Me and Paul always bathed together, usually after Patrick and Karen. Despite it being the season of goodwill and all, there was always time to taunt the life out of him. After spending some time doing the serious stuff in the bath, we ended up seeing who could keep their head under water the longest. I always won as Paul was too honest about keeping the time. By that time the water was getting tepid.

'Oh, dear God, Paul, look at your hands!' I said in horror.

Paul held up his hands to look. 'What's wrong with them?'

'They're covered in wrinkles. You're turning into an old man!'

'Naw I'm not. Naw I'm not,' he cried, searching my eyes for the truth. The tears began to stream out of him.

'Aye, ye are, Paul. Wrinkles is what you get when you're an old man. What are you goin' to do?'

Paul started crying loudly and me da burst in the door.

'What are yous boys at? What's wrong with him?' he asked.

'Look at my hands, Da! Our Tony said I'm turning into an old man,' sobbed Paul.

'I didn't, Da, I didn't. He's just a wee crier,' I pleaded.

'See you, ya wee shite-hawk,' said me da and he hit me a crack on the ear with his open hand. I started crying as well and me ma came through the door.

'Jesus, Mary and Joseph would you look at them two on this good Christmas Eve. Get the two of yous out of that water and get dried for your tea!' she shouted, and stormed back out of the room.

The smell of the fry wafted in from the kitchen. I dried myself and me da dried Paul, who was still sobbing in between laughing at me getting a whack on the ear.

'He's lying, Da,' I said.

'Naw I'm not, Da,' said Paul.

'Shut up the two of yous,' Da said, 'or Santa'll hear ye's and there'll be no presents in the morning!'

The fry was ready by the time we got our pyjamas on. Me da had laid the fire in the hearth in our bedroom ready for us going to bed. Full of excitement after the bath, the wrinkles, the crying and the crack on the ear, we bounded downstairs and into the kitchen, where we all stood around the table – Ma, Da, Karen, Patrick, me and Paul. Colleen was in bed and Glenn was in his cot, too young for Christmas.

The fry consisted of Doherty's sausages, mince, bacon and a fried egg, with tea, bread and butter.

'Who wants high tea?' asked me da.

'Me, me, me, me,' we said in unison. There were no low tea drinkers in our house.

He lifted the teapot about a foot above the mugs and proceeded to pour the tea into each of them. They were already milked. The rust-brown tea poured into the cups through the tea-strainer and splashed when it reached near the top, giving the tea a frothy head. This was high tea. Low tea had no suds. Me da loved doing the high tea.

On the worktop near the cooker the Christmas turkey sat on a baking tray with a chequered tea cloth covering it ready for the oven. When it first arrived at the house it was a full bird, without the feathers, but with its head and all. Me ma had sent us all out to the street while my da went to work on it. When we came back in, me da scared us with his arm, which was reddened and bloodied to the elbow. The turkey had lost its head to make way for the stuffing.

After tea we all went back to the sitting room to watch TV. Val Doonican was on. Me ma and da loved Val Doonican. After a while me da went into the kitchen and brought back two bottles of stout and a metal bottle opener, which he placed in the hearth. Then he returned to the kitchen and brought in two carrots and a slice of Christmas cake on a saucer.

'Are they for Santa and Rudolph the reindeer, Da?' asked Paul, whose wrinkles had almost gone away by this time.

'Aye, that's right, son. That's who they're for. Santa likes his stout … Jesus, did ye's see that?' he called out all of a sudden, pointing out the window at the dark back yard. 'Did ye's see that?'

'What is it, Da? What is it?' we all said, jumping up to see.

'There's Santa on his sleigh over Anne Street!' he said. 'I think it's bedtime for yous before Santa gets here. If he sees yous up, he'll just tell his reindeer to drive on down to Gutsy McGonagle's house and he'll get everything! C'mon quick, up yous get!'

In silent panic we all took to the stairs, hoping that Santa hadn't seen us through the window. When we were all in bed, me da lit the fire in the bedroom hearth. There was no draw from the chimney, so he held a double newspaper page over the front of the fireplace until it caught. He placed the fireguard over the fire, turned off the light and kissed each of us on the forehead before going downstairs.

The darkened room was lit by the cosy red-orange glow from the fire. The Doherty children, filled with bathwater, a fry, Val Doonican and the fear of being awake when Santa came, drifted happily off to sleep.

* * *

Christmas morning came early, though not early enough to save me from Paul, who had peed the bed. We woke in the cold and the damp of it, but it didn't really slow the race – we just changed our yellowy vests and underpants in record-breaking time. When we got downstairs Patrick and Karen were already opening their presents. Me ma and da came down behind us in their nightclothes, rubbing their eyes and yawning. All our names were written on coloured tags attached to the wrapping paper.

My present was wrapped in bright red paper with hundreds of Santas on it. It was a long, thin, rectangular box. I tore off the paper to reveal a ray gun. The box had a picture of a wee boy with a glass space helmet on his head. I opened it and out slid the gun. It had a black butt the same as a cowboy gun, but the barrel was see-through and it had a line of red balls inside about the size of marbles. Our Paul got a large box of Matchbox cars. Everyone got a Mars Christmas stocking; you could see the sweets and chocolate through the white gauze. Patrick had the Spangles out and was eating them. Our Paul started crying.

'That's my gun there so it is,' he cried, pointing at my present. 'I don't want stupid cars!'

'What are ye on about? That's what Santa brought ye, Paul,' said me da, looking puzzled.

'I don't want them. That's mine there – the ray gun.' He sniffled. He was a wild crier.

'Now, boy, pack it in or Santa'll come back and take all away again,' said me ma. 'Jesus, he's always cryin', that boy!'

Paul threw the box of Matchbox cars across the room. They scattered across the floor; some whizzed about the oilcloth. He ran upstairs.

'Sure, Tony'll let ye play with it as well, won't ye, Tony,' shouted me ma after him.

'Aye, Paul, catch yourself on there, boy,' said me da.

'Paul, come on down, I'll let you play with it. We'll go out to the street when it gets light,' I called up to him from the bottom of the stairs, egged on by me ma.

Paul was sitting at the top rubbing his tears and snotters away with his hands. He was easy talked round and lied to. I was the fount of all knowledge as far as he was concerned.

'Will ye, Tony?'

'Aye, c'mon down. It's Christmas!'

Down he came. 'Where's me cars, Da?'

'It's not da, it's daddy,' said me ma.

'All right, Eileen,' said me da. 'Let it go, it's Christmas.'

'Where's me cars?' said Paul again, and we all helped to gather the brilliantly coloured cars from the four corners of the room.

Me da gathered up the torn Christmas paper from the floor and put it in the fire where it briefly cast a bright, multi-coloured illumination over the sitting room.

'Smell them two wi' pish,' said Patrick, looking at me and Paul and holding his nose to exaggerate. New pee doesn't smell that bad. Stale pee does. 'Mammy, g'won get them two washed. They're stinkin'!'

'Aye, I know, Mammy,' said Karen. 'They couldn't go to Mass smelling like that.'

The ray gun was out of the box. It was class.

'Don't fire that gun until I get a look at it,' said me da, taking it off me and going into the kitchen. 'I have to check it first. Get yous two into the bathroom to get washed. Which one of yous peed the bed?'

'It was me, Daddy,' said Paul, red-faced.

'He comes over to my side to pee so his own side is dry. Bloody dribbly drawers!' I said.

Me da placed the ray gun above the high press in the kitchen and ushered us into the bathroom. We were made to stand naked in the empty bath while me da wiped us down like horses with a cloth dipped in a basin of hot water and suds. It was nice and warm at first, but in the freezing cold of the bathroom it turned icy on our skin.

'Here's a towel, son,' he said to me. 'Get yourself dried and upstairs and get dressed. C'mon you over here, Paul. You're next.'

Paul was whimpering in the cold as I ran, shivering, through the kitchen towards the stairs.

After breakfast, me ma and da went upstairs to get dressed. Me and Paul, dressed like catalogue models in our new Christmas clothes, were downstairs with the rest. I grabbed a chair and climbed up to lift down the ray gun from the top of the press.

'C'mon, we'll go out to the street,' I said.

Paul followed obediently in his new clothes. We went across the street towards the waste ground and up the lane towards Moore Street. There was a light covering of snow on the ground. It was freezing cold.

'What'll I shoot?' I asked Paul.

'Shoot that crow there,' he said, pointing up. I put the ray gun to my shoulder, aimed at the hapless bird gliding in the grey sky above and pulled the trigger. The ray gun went off with a space whirr and then a bang. The crow didn't make a sound; it simply dropped from the sky.

'You hit it! You hit it!' Paul called out. 'C'mon to we see.'

We ran around the corner in the direction that the crow fell and came upon the lifeless bird lying sideways on the ground. Its shiny blue-black body was stark against the snow. Paul poked it with a stick and lifted its wing to reveal a bloodied hole underneath.

'Jesus, Tony, ye shot the crow!' he exclaimed in delight.

I stared at the dead crow with a mixture of shock, disbelief and pride. 'That was some shot, hi,' I said and looked at the ray gun and the wee red balls in the barrel with a new sense of wonder and respect. Then I thought, *Is this good or is it bad? And if it's bad, what'll happen? Will I get a hiding for shooting an innocent crow?* It was hard to say. *I didn't know it could fire like that. It's not my fault then.* We stood for a minute or two poking at the bird. Then we heard me da calling us in for Mass.

Our Paul had no doubts that this was great. 'That was some shot, hi,' he said as our house came into view. I wasn't so sure.

'Don't say anything to me ma and da about this, Paul. Right? Ye know me da,' I said.

Me da, Karen and Patrick were gathered at the front door waiting for us in their new clothes, like it was a fashion parade. Karen had a hat on. Me ma was at the door but was staying at home with Colleen and Glenn.

'I hope yous boys haven't destroyed your new clothes,' said me ma. 'C'mere till I see yis.'

'Da, our Tony shot a crow with the ray gun!' Paul proudly informed the gathering. 'Ye wanny see it!'

'Naw, I didn't, Da. It was dead already. It wasn't me.'

'What's he on about?' me da said. 'Give me that out of your hands. I told you not to use it before I looked at it!' He went back into the house with the ray gun and returned a few seconds later.

Away we headed in the snow, the five of us Dohertys, along Hamilton Street towards the Folly and the Long Tower Chapel on the hill. The chapel was packed to the gills and the Mass was just about to start when we arrived at the side door. A choir of angels was singing somewhere within and, leaning either to the left or right, I could see the three life-size kings standing round the Baby Jesus' crib with Mary and Joseph and the life-size donkey, cattle and sheep. All I could think was, *I killed an innocent crow on Christmas morning*.

At long last we heard the strains of 'Gloria in excelsis Deo', with its never-ending chorus of Gloo-oooo-oooo-oooo-rias, and knew we'd escape soon. On the way back home there was still enough snow for me, Paul, Patrick and Karen to slide down the steep Folly ahead of me da. Despite him being careful, he couldn't help sliding down the hill in his shiny black shoes, holding on to the houses to steady himself now and again. On the way back along Hamilton Street, me and Paul went back up to the waste ground to see if the crow was still there. It hadn't moved. It was dead and I had killed it. I'd killed an innocent crow on Christmas morning.

When we reached the house my da opened the front door

and the smell of cooking turkey greeted us. The fire was well-stoked and the sitting room was warm. Me ma was sitting on the black plastic sofa, but she looked unhappy. She had the Quality Street tin beside her. It was full of shiny wrappers.

'Who ate all the sweets?' she asked. 'There's not one left,' she added, looking at me da.

No one spoke. The only sound was from the coals shifting in the fire and wee Glenn gurgling in his cot over at the Christmas tree lights.

'I've never seen a crowd like yis,' she said, turning her head away in disappointment.

I went over and sat down beside her on the black plastic sofa. 'I took some, Mammy. But I didn't take them all. I'm sorry.'

'At least you're honest, Tony,' she said, looking at the other three in the line-up.

'I took some,' said Patrick, with a shy grin.

'So did I, Mammy,' said Karen. 'It was me who wrapped the tin again in Sellotape.'

I started crying into my hands. 'This is the worst Christmas ever!'

'For fuck's sake, Tony, it's only a few sweeties!' said me da from the scullery door.

'It's not the sweets, Da. I shot an innocent crow with the ray gun. I shot an innocent crow on Christmas morning!' I said, still crying.

Me da burst out laughing and went into the scullery and closed the door. A few seconds later he came out again with the ray gun in one hand and his other hand behind his back.

'You'll shoot no more crows with that,' he said, handing me the gun. The red balls had been removed and the barrel was now an empty plastic tube.

'And here yous go! This'll shut all your crying mouths!' he said and produced an open tin of Roses. 'Happy Christmas!'

And so it was.

10

THIS MAN'S WEE BOY

January 1972.

> Armoured cars and tanks and guns
> Came to take away our sons.
> But every man must stand behind
> The men behind the wire.

Me da came back from a demonstration on Magilligan Strand with a record, a single, of 'The Men Behind the Wire' by The Barleycorn. He came in the door soaking wet with the record under his arm. Our record player was in the front room, the fancy room with the tin shield covering the window. The light had to be on all the time if you were in the room. We went in and played the record with the sound turned up loud. Me ma and da stayed in the sitting room, where it was warm. After a while I went back into the sitting room as well. They stopped talking when I came in. Me da was sitting smoking a Park Drive. His speckled coat with the black fur collar was draped over a chair near the blazing fire. Steam was rising from it and there were two small puddles on the oilcloth where the rain had dripped down from the ends of the sleeves. I went and sat on the floor near the fire. Me ma and da were sitting at opposite ends of the sofa with an orange-cushioned gap between them.

'How did you get back from Magilligan?' I asked after a minute of silence.

'There was a bus organised,' me da replied.

'Why did they organise a protest on a beach?'

'Because that's where the internees are being kept. In Magilligan Prison.'

'They have a prison on a beach?' *That's some place for a prison*, I thought.

'Your daddy went down to see if he could see your uncle Joe,' said me ma, looking at me da. 'Your uncle Joe joined the British Army and your daddy went down to see if he could talk some sense into him.'

'My uncle Joe's in the British Army?' I said in disbelief. 'Why'd he do that?' The last time I'd seen him he was living down in Chamberlain Street, behind the Rossville Street flats. Me da took us there one day.

'I don't know, son. He didn't tell anyone. He just left and went to England,' said me da. 'The next thing we knew he'd joined the army.'

'And did you see him the day at Magilligan?' I asked.

'Naw, he wasn't there – at least, I didn't see him. It was his regiment, though. The Parachute Regiment.'

'Does anyone else know he's in the British Army?' I asked, suddenly worried that we would be the talk of the street.

'What do you mean?' asked me da.

'He means are we going to be a laughing stock because Joe's in the British Army,' me ma said – a wee bit accusing, I thought.

'Nobody else knows,' me da said.

They still didn't seem to want to talk much so I got up from the floor and went back into the front room to learn the words of 'The Men Behind the Wire' with the rest of them. I said nothing about Uncle Joe. For all I knew he was one of the BA who dragged fathers from their beds or who beat sons while helpless mothers watched the blood pour from their heads. 'Armoured cars and tanks and guns.' We sang until the words became the new mantra among the families in the street.

* * *

The following Saturday I was sent out to the back yard to get a bucket of coal for the fire. It was getting dark and it was freezing cold, too cold even to play in the street. I placed the coal bucket on the ground beside the hatch of the coal bunker and had just slid the shovel into the hatch when a huge rat darted out between my feet. I let out a squeal and jumped up to squat on the edge of the coal bunker. I could hear its claws scrape on the hard ground as it dashed to the bottom of the yard and escaped out through a wee hole in the back gate. I hated rats. I wished we had a dog like Dandy McKinney. She'd be shaking the life out of it by now and tossing it into the air. I wondered why we didn't have our own dog.

To be sure that there were no more rats, I lifted the bunker lid to look in. All I could see was black lumps of coal, heaped to a point in the middle where the coalman had dumped it. I had to use my two hands to carry the bucket back into the sitting room. Me da took it off me with one hand, placed it down beside the hearth and set about lighting the fire. The ashes from the night before were shovelled onto a few sheets of the *Derry Journal* and wrapped up. Then me da asked me to take them to the bin in the yard.

'I don't wanny, Da. A big mausey rat was in the coal bunker and it scared the shite out of me.'

'You scared of a wee rat, hi?' he said, teasing me.

'Aye, but it was a big mauser, Da!' I said, my hands held apart to show its size. 'Its tail was that size!' I said, widening the gap between my hands.

'All right, I'll take them out,' he said and took the parcel out to the bin.

'Close that door behind you,' called me ma after him. 'I don't want any rats running through the house!'

'God, it would founder you out there,' said me da when he came back in.

Me da used crumpled up newspapers, sticks and half-burnt coals from the night before to light the fire in the sitting room. Scrunched-up paper was arranged at the bottom, the sticks were set on top of the paper, followed by last night's coals and some fresh coal. The hall door had to be open for the draught. Our Paul pulled the hall door after him one time when me da was lighting the fire and the whole room filled with smoke.

'Do yous want the fire lit in your room the night?' he asked us wains when he'd got the fire in the sitting room going.

'Aye, Da, that would be great.'

We all loved the fire going in the bedroom.

Me da took all he needed up to our bedroom to get our wee fire ready. I carried the sticks up for him. The hearth in our room was smaller than the sitting-room fire, and the fireplace was made of dull brown tiles. He laid the fire but didn't light it.

'I'll light it after seven. No point heating an empty room,' he said, and we went back downstairs.

'Nearly time for your baths,' called me ma from the kitchen. 'Karen, you bath on your own the night.'

'Why's Karen having a bath on her own?' asked Patrick.

'Because she's bigger now,' said me da.

'But so am I,' said Patrick, getting up from the sofa to show his height. He was as tall as Karen.

'Just never mind,' said me ma. 'Karen, your bath's running. Get yourself ready.'

Karen got her bath first and then Patrick went in on his own. Me and Paul went in afterwards. Me da topped the water up a bit with a kettle full of boiling water. The bathroom was freezing so we scrubbed quickly in the warm, soapy water and then stood up in it to get dried.

'Let me see your hands, Paul,' I said.

Paul studied his hands for wrinkles.

'Ha! Caught you!'

'Shut up, you,' said me da, laughing. 'No narking the night.'

Once we were dry we ran through the kitchen and sitting room in the nude to go upstairs to put our pyjamas on.

'Would ye look at them two,' laughed me ma as we flashed past her. 'Like two whippet pups!'

When we came down for our Saturday night fry, Karen and Patrick were glued to the TV. There was a group singing 'Beg, Steal or Borrow'. It was Britain's entry in the *Eurovision Song Contest*, played on the *Cliff Richard Show*, so I instantly hated it. Our Patrick said Cliff Richard talked as if he had his balls in his mouth. The TV reception wasn't great and we called me da in to look at it. He lifted the aerial with the two antennae from the top of the TV and took it to the windowsill, but it didn't make any difference so he banged the side of the TV with his hand and did the same on the other side. Still no difference.

'It must be a valve going. I'll have to see about getting it fixed next week,' he said.

It was watchable though; we could still make out most of what was going on.

Because it was cold and we had only two chairs at the kitchen table, we were allowed to bring our fries into the sitting room, balancing the plates on our knees while our mugs of tea sat on the floor at our feet. Doherty's sausages, mince, black pudding, potato bread and a fried egg with tea, bread and butter. By this time the fire was well caught so the hall door could be closed to keep the heat in and we all sat eating our fry and suffering Cliff Richard on the blurry TV.

I found myself trying to imagine Uncle Joe in a British Army uniform, and wondered how he could join them after seeing what they had done in our streets and houses. *What would we tell people if the IRA shot him dead?* Jesus, I didn't know!

'Da, can we stay up to watch *Match of the Day* the night?' asked Paul. I had said to him when we were in the bath to ask me da. It had worked before.

'Aye, if yous are good and yous behave yourselves.'

'Great! I hope Leeds is on,' said Paul.

'Leeds are shite, so they are,' I said.

Patrick wasn't interested in football. Only me, Paul and me da. Me da supported Man United. In the summer he'd bought me a Man United jersey. I hated Man United by then, but loved the idea of looking like Georgie Best, and I wore it when we played football a few times out the Daisy Field.

'Watch your language, boy,' said me da.

'All right, Leeds are a pile of brown mess,' I said.

'That's better,' he said with a smile.

The strains of 'The Men Behind the Wire' drifted in over the sound of the TV from the front room, where Karen and Patrick had gone. I followed shortly afterwards because I wanted to learn the song. The song was important because it was written in support of the internees, as the prisoners were called. I didn't know why. That's all me da told us. They were internees, interned without a fair trial. Patrick and Karen knew the words already. I needed to catch up. The front room was freezing. It had a hearth but the fire was never lit.

> Proudly march behind our banners,
> Firmly stand behind our men.
> We will have them free to help us,
> Build a nation once again.

Later in the evening, before *Match of the Day* came on, we were all in the sitting room enjoying the warmth when me da reached down beside the sofa and brought out a brown-paper bag filled with old shoes. He kept all the old worn shoes that couldn't be handed down to burn in the fire in the winter.

'Oh great, Daddy, you're goin' to burn the shoes,' said Paul. We loved burning the shoes.

'Aye, son. That's right. It's that time again,' said me da,

placing an old pair of his own on the fire, heels down and toes up with the sole facing out. They started to burn right away and me da lifted the fireguard and placed it over the fire. After a few minutes they were blazing, giving off orangey-blue and green flames, different from the orange and red of the coals. The room filled with the dancing light, and the heat made us drowsy. Paul nodded off on the sofa and the rest of us struggled to keep our eyes open.

Just as *Match of the Day* was about to start, I saw me da looking round at us, splayed out on the sofa and chairs in various stages of sleepiness. I sat up and forced my eyes open, but it was too late.

'Okay, wains, it's pollyfookie time,' said me da, meaning for us to get up the stairs. 'Yous are all knackered and we're for early Mass in the morning. C'mon you, Paul.'

He reached down to the sofa and lifted Paul up over his shoulder to take him out to the toilet for a pee. I followed. Me da had to hold Paul up beside the toilet to pee because he had his eyes closed already. Both of us peed together into the toilet at the same time. If Paul had have been awake we would have had a pee-race to see who finished first. Me da lifted Paul up again and went upstairs ahead of me. The fire had been lit earlier in our room and it was nice and warm.

'Pull them blankets back there, Tony, till I put him in,' said me da and he laid Paul down on the bed. 'Jesus, this young fella's a ton weight.' He stood up, holding the bottom of his back with both hands. 'He's too big for me to lift now.'

I climbed into bed beside Paul and pulled the covers up over us.

'Okay, night night, wee Dohertys,' said me da and he turned off the light.

'Night night, Daddy,' I said back and out he went, pulling the door closed behind him.

As we drifted off to sleep, the room glowed red from the fire and threw slow-moving shadows on the bedroom wall.

I woke in the middle of the night needing to do a pee. I lay in bed, afraid to get up. After a while I nudged Paul to see if he was awake. No response.

'Paul!' I whispered right into his ear. 'Are you wakened?'

He just gave a sleepy grunt and I knew there was no chance of him getting up with me. I persevered.

'Paul, have you to pee?' I whispered, pushing his shoulders, hoping his bladder would force him awake like mine had.

No joy. He was dead to the world. The image of the big mausey rat scarpering out of the coal bunker filled my head. I lay on for a while and tried to get back to sleep, but the pee in my bladder wanted to come out and it was getting painful. I got out of bed and went out onto the landing. I thought about knocking on me ma and da's door to see if one of them would come downstairs with me, but both Colleen and Glenn were in there as well and I'd get killed if I woke them.

I stood at the top of the landing and stepped down the first few stairs before the turn at the landing window. Looking down, I saw that the door to the front room was open. In my mind all I could see was a huge, grey rat with a long, pink tail sitting behind the door waiting for me to go past. I couldn't go any further. I was scared stiff and I could feel the pee about to come out. I hated that room already because of the tin shield over the window; now there was a huge mausey rat in it! I went back upstairs to the landing window. All I could see outside was darkness and the lights of Creggan in the distance. I went back down a couple of stairs, but the thought of the rat was too great and I went back to the top of the stairs, moaning and crying under my breath in case I woke anyone. I couldn't handle the pain any more. I pulled down my underpants and peed all over the stairs. I knew if I peed in one spot there would be a puddle for days. So I spread the pee around and pushed it out till it hit the bottom of the stairs; I kept the dribbles for the top stairs. With a bit of luck it would be dry in the morning, I thought. I went back to bed greatly relieved and tucked back into the warmth beside Paul.

* * *

The marlies were freezing in my hands. We kept them in our pockets and only took one or two out at a time to play. The wee net bags with the colourful cardboard tops had appeared in Melaugh's shop the previous week and we'd spent our pay on them on Friday night when me da came home from work. He paid me and Paul at the front door where we were waiting and we ran full speed up the street to Melaugh's. It was a race and I beat our Paul to the shop door. Every boy in the street and far beyond was into marbles now.

Me, Johnny Barbour, Dooter, Paddy Brown and our Paul were playing just outside our house. We had tried to prise chewing gum from the footpath with our fingernails but it was frozen solid.

'Get a butter knife,' said Paddy, and I went into the kitchen and got one.

The house was dark and there was no one in. I came out with the knife and poked at the large white patch of flattened chewing gum; eventually it came free of the freezing flagstones in small, hard slices. There was enough to share so we all got a piece, kissed it up to God and put it in our mouths. It wasn't long before the heat in my mouth softened the chewing gum to reveal the minty taste of Beechnut. We chewed gently, sieving out the dirt and grit with our tongues and front teeth.

The bright winter sunlight was beginning to fade and was soon replaced by the light of the street lamps.

'Will we get a game of boodlies?' said Paddy.

There was nothing else to do. The marlie circle was gouged out with the butter knife from the dry, frozen muck just below the kerb and we gathered round the circle on our hunkers to pitch into it. Each of us had green snotters dripping from our noses with the cold, which we licked, snorted up or wiped on our hardened sleeves. I threw my marlie first. The marlie flew wrongly from my cold fingers and skidded on the hard muck and out of the circle.

'My fingers are freezing. I have to get another go,' I said and tossed another into the ring.

No one objected. It was easier this time and the marlie stayed in. I threw my fist in the air and pretended to smoke a fag in satisfaction, blowing out a long puff of frosty air as smoke.

'Right, Dooter, throw your boodlie!' I said.

He threw his marlie and it stayed in the ring.

'Yessss!' said Dooter, as if he had scored a goal in football. He wiped his snottery nose on his sleeve in satisfaction.

'There's Fuck-a-dee,' said Paddy Brown, and we turned to see Eff-a-dee come out of his house, his hand stuck to his mouth and him grinning behind it. His da followed. They didn't come over to us. Eff-a-dee just sat on his windowsill, watching and grinning. His da stood at the door.

'My turn,' said our Paul and he threw his marlie into the ring. It stayed in. 'Yes!' he cried and all eyes fell on Paddy Brown.

Paddy was a brilliant marlie player. He wiped his snotters on his sleeve, sucking them up his nostrils at the same time, and stood up from his hunkers. He bent over, swung his throwing hand between his legs and tossed his marlie in, hitting mine and knocking it out of the ring. It scooted along on the frozen muck and fell down the grating, gone for ever.

'Jammy balls!' I said, angered at getting knocked out and losing the marlie for good.

'Jammy balls, me hole! That was the shot of the century!' said Paddy.

'Who's jammy balls?' said Gutsy, approaching from his house and tapping his bulging pocket full of marlies. 'Yous'll see a bit of class now!'

'Hi, John,' he called over to Eff-a-dee. 'You wanny play?' Eff-a-dee looked back, grinning, and stood up from the windowsill.

'Is it my turn or what?' said Gutsy, turning his back on Eff-a-dee, who was coming towards us.

Gutsy put a marlie in his mouth, took it out, dried it on his trousers and rolled it between his finger and thumb. Then he flicked it with his thumb and it landed cleanly in the ring, knocking Paddy Brown's out with a sharp crack.

'Fuck!' said Paddy.

'Fuck is right,' said Gutsy. 'You're out to fuck!' and he bent to lift Paddy's marlie.

'I want back in again,' I said and stood up from my hunkers to throw.

'Your da's been shot, hi,' said Gutsy, as I was about to throw.

Something shifted within me between my heart and my gut. I put my hand on it. If anyone had news to bring it would be Gutsy. My mouth went dry, and the Beechnut I was chewing became hard and tasteless. I spat it out on the road. I looked at our Paul but he hadn't heard Gutsy. He was distracted by Eff-a-dee coming over to us.

'What? How would *you* know?' I said to Gutsy.

'Fuck-a-dee,' said Eff-a-dee, grinning, now part of our circle around the ring. Our Paul and Johnny were laughing with him.

'He was shot down the Bog,' said Gutsy. 'I saw him getting carted into an ambulance.' He popped another marlie into his mouth.

'You be good now, John. No cursing or I'll bring you in again,' said Eff-a-dee's da from his front door across the street.

'Gutsy, I'm goney batter the shite out of you for telling me lies!' I said, sort of realising how ridiculous the threat sounded under the circumstances. I had no choice. He *was* telling lies.

'I'm not. I swear to God, hi,' he said, hurriedly blessing his heart with his marlie hand.

'Fuck-a-dee, fuck-a-dee,' said Eff-a-dee excitedly, a marble in his hand.

Paul, Johnny and Paddy Brown were laughing.

From the corner of my eye I noticed the figure of Kathleen McCallion approaching our house. Kathleen was married to me da's cross-eyed cousin, Paddy McCallion from Quarry Street. Kathleen walked past us without a word and went into our house. The front door was open. Strange, I thought, what would she be looking for?

'Gutsy, you're gettin' it after we come out later on,' I said and got up to go in. I had the butter knife in my hand.

Gutsy got back on his hunkers, ready to throw another marlie.

I walked into the hallway and pulled the front door behind me. *That Gutsy's a wee effing shite*, I thought to myself. *I'll kick the shite out of him later for telling lies.* But a wee voice in my head was saying that it might not be a lie. Why would he lie about such a thing? And what was Kathleen doing in our house on a Sunday? She's hardly ever in our house. I walked through the sitting room and Kathleen was in the kitchen busying herself. The kitchen was already tidy. We had all cleaned it up after the Sunday dinner earlier on, before me ma and da went out to the march with their big coats on.

Kathleen heard me coming in and pretended she didn't. She was wiping the sink with a cloth made from old knickers. I went through to the toilet, did a pee and came back into the kitchen. Kathleen was still standing at the sink with her back to me. She didn't look at me once. I took in her dirty fair hair and her flowery apron tied in a bow behind her waist. *I wonder why she came to our house with her apron on*, I thought.

'Kathleen, is me da shot?' The words rang out round the

cold kitchen and sounded as if someone else had said them.

Kathleen stiffened at the sink with the cloth still in her hand. She said nothing. She didn't turn round. I stood on, wondering if she had heard me.

After a few seconds she said, 'It'll be all right, Tony. Go you back out to the street to play.' There was a flat emptiness in her voice. She still hadn't turned around to face me.

I know it's true. I know, I said to myself. *But she didn't say it was true and she's a grown woman.* I knew then, but I didn't know. *It couldn't be true because no grown-up has told me so.* We'd only had our dinner a couple of hours ago. Meat, spuds, peas and gravy. They'd gone out together with their big coats on. *They'll be back shortly, me ma and da, from the march.*

I went back into the sitting room. The house was freezing as the fire hadn't been lit yet. I went and stood out in the hall. The front door had blown open and I could see our Paul, Johnny, Paddy Brown, Gutsy and Eff-a-dee playing in the frozen muck at the kerb. It couldn't be true. *Sure, isn't everyone out still playing boodlies?* I sat at the bottom of the carpeted stairs, examining its pattern and colour between my feet and scuffing it with my shoes to see if I could change it any. I remembered what had happened in the middle of the night and felt the backside of my trousers to see if it was wet with pee. It wasn't. The pee must've dried in. I touched the carpet with my fingers and it felt dry. There was no smell either.

Looking up, I could see it was all but dark outside. The

marlie game was still going on in the streetlight. Kathleen was now in the sitting room on her knees cleaning out the ashes from the grate. I knew. I knew. But I didn't know. No one except Gutsy had told me and he was the same age as me. He didn't count. I rubbed the feeling in my gut with my hand to see if it would go away. It didn't. I just sat on the stairs and hoped that what I thought I knew wasn't true.

After a short while my granda Connor came through the front door in his long, dark-grey overcoat buttoned to the neck. I hadn't seen him since he'd taken me down the town after my birthday and bought me a brand new pair of Gola football boots. They were black with golden stripes on the sides. He wanted me to be a footballer and play for Ireland. So did I. After we'd got the boots in McLaughlin's shoe shop we'd gone to Tracey's Bar in William Street, where he drank pints and pints of stout. I got crisps and Coke. His friends all wanted to see my new football boots and gave me money.

'Hello, son,' he said as he approached me on the stairs.

I stood up to see if there was anyone following him in through the door. There wasn't.

'Hello, Granda.'

Granda Connor went slowly past me into the sitting room where Kathleen was and closed the door behind him. I could hear them whispering but couldn't make out what they were saying. After a few minutes he came out and, without looking at me, stood at the front door looking up and down the street.

His tall bulk blocked the sight and lessened the sound from the street. His slicked-back, jet-black hair shone under the bare light in the hall.

Our Paul called to him from the street. 'Hi, Granda, we're playing boodlies. Our Tony got knocked out!'

Granda Connor said, 'Ach, sure there you go. Sure Tony's goney be a footballer when he grows up. Isn't that right, Tony?' he asked, half turning around to me.

'Aye, Granda,' I said from the stairs.

Granda Connor stood on in the frame of the front door. A man with grey hair and a red nose approached him, spoke in whispers, came into the house past me and went into the sitting room, closing the door behind him.

Our Karen arrived at the front door in an agitated rush. 'Granda, Granda, a wee girl up the street told me that me daddy's dead – that he's been shot!'

'It's all right, Karen. It's all right,' said me granda. He had his hands on her shoulders.

'G'won you, tell her it's not true, Granda. There she is there – look!' She pointed up towards Melaugh's shop.

'You mind your own business!' me granda called up the street to the wee girl. 'I'll put me toe up your arse if you come down here.'

'But it's not true, Granda! Isn't it not?' cried Karen.

Granda Connor pulled Karen into him and held her without saying anything else. Karen was crying into his overcoat.

He hasn't told her it was true, I thought, still hanging on. *He hasn't told her it's true.* I knew. I knew. But I didn't know. No one, other than Gutsy, had said it.

Then Karen ran into the house and up the stairs past me. Her face was streaked with tears. I could feel the cold from her clothes as she passed. She ran into me ma and da's bedroom and banged the door closed. *Sure me granda didn't tell her it was true.* I looked at him, still filling the front door. I hadn't the nerve to ask him anything in case he told me what I didn't want to hear. I sat with my head down and looked at the carpet. I was hanging on to the only hope I had.

A woman with blonde hair came into the house past me granda. She looked at me sitting on the stairs, smiled and went through the sitting room into the kitchen. She left the door open. They were whispering in the kitchen, the three of them. The fire was lit in the sitting room by this time. Then a small woman with dark hair came into the house and went into the sitting room. The ones in the kitchen joined her and they all just sat there. Karen came back down the stairs and went through the sitting room into the kitchen. No one spoke to her and she came back out after a short while. A few people had gathered around the front door to talk to me granda.

Our Patrick came in from the street. 'What are you doing sitting there?' he asked me.

I just shrugged. To explain the real reason would be to acknowledge that there could be something badly wrong;

it would increase the chances of it being true. I just looked down at the stair carpet. Patrick stood at the door to the sitting room and asked Karen what was going on. I didn't hear her answer; I don't think she said anything. The people in the sitting room said nothing. They avoided our eyes and looked at one another.

A car pulled up just past the front door. It could have been a taxi. Granda Connor moved away from the front door towards it; then a crowd of people appeared to gather all at once in the space he left. Me ma was in the lead, and Granda Connor had Paul by the hand. I stood up on the stairs as people filed into the hall behind them, searching their faces for me da's. My eyes darted from person to person but he wasn't there. It was only aunts, uncles and neighbours. Me ma passed me without looking at me and stopped at the sitting room door. The house was completely silent.

'Your daddy's dead. He was shot by the army,' she said.

I dropped back down on the stairs and put my head in my hands. I started to cry and I sat there rubbing my eyes.

'The bastards! The bastards! The fuckin' bastards,' screamed our Patrick from the sitting room.

'There now, Patrick. There now,' said me ma, pulling him close to her. She sat on the sofa and Patrick was on her lap. He was crying hard into her chest.

'I want our Paddy back! I want our Paddy back!' screamed Aunt Siobhán.

'You can't have him back! For God's sake woman, he's dead!' me granda shouted at her.

'Jesus, Connor, let her say what she wants,' said the man with the red nose in a half whisper. 'She's in shock.'

'I'm sorry, Siobhán,' said me granda and he started crying into his large hands. 'I don't know what to say.' He wiped his eyes and nose with a white handkerchief. Karen was clinging on to him and crying into his overcoat.

The hall was bunged with people, mostly aunts, uncles and neighbours, and no one could get in or out.

'C'mon over here, Tony,' me ma called from the sofa.

I got up and squeezed through to sit beside her. I put my head down on her lap. Patrick was still pressed into her chest, cursing away to himself.

'Mammy, where's me da now?' I asked.

'He's over in the morgue. In Altnagelvin.'

'Were you over? Did you see him?'

'Aye, I did, Tony,' she said with a heavy sigh.

I could tell she didn't want to say any more, so I didn't ask any more questions. I just sat there and let her rub my head and shoulders with her hand. She didn't cry like everyone else.

'There's thirteen dead,' said a man's voice. I looked up and saw it was the man with the red nose.

Me da's cousin, Paddy McCallion, came through the sitting-room door. He knelt down in front of me ma in his well-worn, shiny brown suit, his long black hair sticking out all over the place as if he'd been in a fight.

'Jesus, Eileen, they've killed our Paddy. They've killed our Paddy.' He had her hand in both of his.

Everyone in the sitting room was watching.

'I know, Paddy. He's gone for ever,' said me ma.

'Jesus, Eileen, what are we goney do? They're saying there's thirteen dead. Thirteen! Jesus!' Paddy sounded almost hysterical.

'I don't know, Paddy. I just don't know,' me ma said with a long sigh.

'They'll have to pay for this. The bastards!' he said, and with that he got up and rushed out of the room into the hall.

Me ma nodded to someone to follow him out. 'Make sure he doesn't do anything. There's murder round at the Mex,' she said.

'Ma, how are we goney live without me da?' I asked. 'We're not goney have any money to live.'

Me ma laughed and said, 'Ach, Tony, don't you be thinking like that. It'll be all right. Don't worry. Did you hear him, Daddy?'

'The bastards! The bastards! The fuckin bastards!' It was our Patrick again, screaming.

He's a wild curser, I thought, as me ma held me on the sofa. *He's too young to be cursing like that.*

* * *

The long, black hearse pulled up in front of the house. We were all gathered at our door and there was a large crowd in the street. Chesty Crossan was standing outside his cottage across from us, his eyes red from crying. I'd never seen Chesty cry before. Eff-a-dee and his da were standing beside him. Eff-a-dee had his hand up to his mouth and was grinning at people.

Me da's coffin was carried into the house and into the front room. Me ma brought us all into the room, just her and the six wains. Everyone else stayed outside. The smoked glass door was closed. Someone had taken the tin screen off the front window and daylight came through the orange curtains, giving the room an unnaturally warm glow. We gathered around the coffin. The lid had been taken off and we could see me da's face with his eyes closed. His black moustache stood out from his white, waxy face. He had a small round hole right between the eyes. I was standing right beside his head.

'Is that where me daddy was shot?' I asked me ma, almost in a whisper. She was standing with Glenn in her arms at me da's feet.

'Naw. That must be just a cut when he fell. He was shot in the back – they shot him in the back.'

'Is me daddy up in heaven already?' asked Colleen. She was nearly three.

We laughed.

'Aye, I'm sure he is,' me ma said, smiling back at her. 'Do yous want to touch him?' she asked.

We took turns at touching his hands. They were icy cold. His fingers were entwined with a set of black Rosary beads. The smoky, bronze stains had gone from the fingers of his right hand, as had the black dirt under his fingernails. His hands had been scrubbed clean.

I'm going to miss your smoky, brown fingers, I said in my head to me da. *And your Park Drive.*

There were long periods of silence while we stood and looked at me da, and looked at me ma, and looked at one another. Karen was crying into her hands and hugged me ma and Glenn. Patrick cried too, and me and Paul stood near me da's face and touched his jet-black hair.

* * *

During the wake period I was sent to Melaugh's shop for messages. I had a list of things to get with a fiver inside the note: sixty Embassy Red, forty Park Drive, a loaf, sliced ham and sliced cheese. I walked up the street on my own and went in the shop door. Paddy Melaugh was standing behind the till; his wife came in through the door connecting the shop to their house. As I walked up to the counter Paddy half-turned to his wife and said something that I didn't hear. Mrs Melaugh looked at me across the counter, looked back at Paddy and nodded her head.

'You all right, son?' asked Paddy.

Mrs Melaugh didn't say anything. She just looked on.

'Gimme sixty Embassy Red, forty Park Drive, a loaf, eight slices of ham and eight thin slices of cheese,' I said, adding, 'Here's the note.' I slid the note across the faded pale-blue counter towards him. I couldn't help but notice the bags of marlies lined up in rows on the counter along with loaves of Hunter's bread, boxes of Dainties, Chocolate Logs, Whoppers and jars of lollipops and coloured sweets. Paddy lifted the note and studied it. Mrs Melaugh stayed in the doorway and smiled at me when I looked at her.

'Right. Sixty Embassy Red.' He lifted three twenty-packs from the shelf behind him and placed them on the counter in front of me. Then he lifted two boxes of Park Drive and placed them beside the Embassy Reds.

'Ham and cheese. Eight each,' he said, reading aloud from the note. 'Your daddy likes the hard chee–' He stopped himself too late but carried on as if nothing had happened, loading a large, rectangular block of cheese onto the cutting machine. He pressed a button on its side and it began to whirr. He then counted the slices of cheese as they fell onto the paper below: 'One ... two ... three ... four ... five ... six ... seven ... and eight. That's the cheese.' He turned the cutter off, wrapped the cheese up and placed it beside the fag boxes.

'Now the ham,' he said, more to himself than to anyone else. He lifted the block of cheese away and replaced it with a mound of crumbed ham in an orange net, which he pulled back with his fingers at one end. He adjusted something on the cutter and switched it back on with a whirr.

'One ... two ... three ... four ... five ... six ... seven ... and eight. That's the ham,' he said and turned the cutter off. While it slowly came to a stop, he wrapped the ham and placed it beside the rest of the messages. 'And here's your loaf!' he said, lifting the bread from the pile on the counter. 'You'll need a wee bag.'

'Naw, Paddy, it's okay. I'll just carry them home,' I said.

'Ach naw, son – a wee bag sure.' He reached below the counter and brought out a used brown paper bag. He put each item in the bag before folding it at the top.

'There you go, son,' said Paddy, sliding the bag over to me. 'And take this here as well.' He wrapped the fiver back up in the note and slid it towards me.

'Thank you, Mr Melaugh,' I said. 'Churrio, Mrs Melaugh.'

'Churrio, son,' she called back from the doorway.

I turned to leave and Paddy called out: 'Hi, wee Doherty! C'mere over before you go.' I looked round. Paddy was beckoning me over with his hand.

I walked back to the counter. Mrs Melaugh was standing beside Paddy behind the counter. Both of them had tears running down their faces; Paddy had taken his thick glasses off to wipe his eyes.

Mrs Melaugh lifted three bags of marbles from the counter and said, 'Here, open your bag, son.' She put the marbles in on top of the other messages. 'These are for you and your two brothers.'

'Thanks, Paddy. Thanks, Mrs Melaugh,' I said, and turned to leave again.

'God bless you, son,' I heard her say as the shop door closed behind me.

As I walked down Hamilton Street on that cold, bright afternoon there was a long line of people outside our house. *Two bags for me and one for Paul*, I thought to myself. *Our Patrick doesn't play marlies*. But the nearer I got to the house the more generous I became. *I'll give the other bag to Gutsy, or maybe Eff-a-dee*, I thought, as I squeezed past the orderly queue of wake-goers lined up in our hallway.

* * *

It lashed with rain on the day of the funeral. It drummed on the black sea of umbrellas as we followed me ma and granda up the steps of Saint Mary's Chapel in Creggan. Inside the chapel we walked up the aisle together as a family. As we were being ushered into a pew by a man wearing a white armband I caught sight of the long line of wooden coffins, laid out in a row, stretching the whole width of the altar. I wondered which one was me da's. They all looked the same from where we sat. I watched other families coming up the aisle and being seated in front and behind us. Everyone was soaking wet and the sound of crying echoed around the chapel. The place hummed with sadness, disbelief, pity, shock, all at once. Me ma and me granda looked lost, and me granda's eyes were red.

The Mass began. I heard nothing but the rain bucketing down outside. I felt nothing but cold and wet inside. When the Mass was over we were ushered back down the aisle and outside the chapel. The rain was still pouring out of the heavens. We followed the hearse as it moved slowly towards the cemetery below. Everyone was wearing black and when you looked up all you could see was the undersides of black umbrellas with the odd bit of grey sky in between. There were people on both sides of the road looking at us as we passed with our heads bowed.

When we reached the cemetery the procession slowed down even more as it was packed with people. We eventually found our way to the graveside where me da's coffin was placed beside the newly dug grave. The rain pelted off it, and the grassy verges had turned to muck and puddles. A row of freshly dug graves lay to each side of me da's. We all stood as near the graveside as we could get – me ma and granda, us brothers and sisters, me aunts and uncles and cousins. The black umbrellas were still up and the water dripped from them onto our heads and shoulders. Despite the lashing rain, you could still make out the sound of people crying; it ebbed and flowed in waves on the wind.

'C'mon you away o' that, son.'

I felt a hand on my shoulder and looked up to see a man wearing a white armband, and a sea of faces looking on behind him. I hesitated and was about to come away at his beckoning when me ma turned, white-faced with her black veil blowing up over her black hat, towards us from the graveside.

'It's okay, mister. That's this man's wee boy,' she said, pulling me over to her side, where her thick black coat felt cold and damp.

GLOSSARY

alroyt	English regional pronunciation of 'all right' (possibly in a Midlands accent)
BA	British Army
blatter	move noisily, with a clatter
bluttered	severely drunk
bob	shilling
boys-a-boys	colloquial: 'oh, dear me!'
brock	from the Irish *broc* meaning refuse or rubbish
cacked	messed or excreted
can't take your oil	someone can't accept when they are beaten
dander	walk or meander
dear bye it	(someone will) pay dearly for something (a threat)
deef	deaf
dootsy	staid
fleadh (n.)	Irish for celebration or feast, pronounced 'fla'
foundered	freezing or frozen
gis	'give me' something ('give us')
houl	hold
hunkers	haunches
marlies (also boodlies)	marbles

mauser/mausey	a huge thing/huge
messages	errands
mizzle	light rain, drizzle
moyt	English regional pronunciation of 'mate' (possibly in a Midlands accent)
mucker	friend
nark (v. & n.)	v. to aggravate or tease; n. someone who does this
oul	old or unwanted
piece (n.)	a slice of bread
po	chamber pot
poke	a 'poke' in common Derry language is an ice-cream
press	a cupboard or dresser
riddley gun	machine gun
rift and pish	burp and pee
royfil	English regional pronunciation of 'rifle' (possibly in a Midlands accent)
slabber	slaver, dribble
steever	a good kick
swiddies	sweets
themuns	those people
thon	that
tig	a children's chase game, also known as tag
tilled	ajar
wain	baby or child, possibly from 'wee one'
wile	from wild, meaning terrible
yis	see 'yous'
yous	referring to more than one person